Gazophylacii Naturae Et Artis Decas Prima

GAZOPHYLACII
NATURÆ & ARTIS
DECAS PRIMA.

In quâ ANIMALIA, QUADRUPEDA, AVES, PISCES, REPTILIA, INSECTA, VEGETABILIA; Item FOSSILIA, Corpora MARINA & STIRPES MINERALES è *Terra* eruta, LAPIDES figurâ infignes &c.

DESCRIPTIONIBUS brevibus & ICONIBUS illuftrantur.

Hifce Annexa erit *Supellex* ANTIQUARIA, NUMISMATA, GEMMÆ excifæ, & fculpturæ, Opera Figulina, Lucernæ, Urnæ, Inftrumenta varia, INSCRIPTIONES, BUSTA, reliquaque ad rem prifcam fpectantia : Item MACHINÆ, EFFIGIES clarorum virorum, omniaque ARTE producta.

PATRONIS fuis & MOECENATIBUS

D. D. D.

JACOBUS PETIVER.

LONDINI:

Ex Officinâ *Chrift. Bateman* ad infignia *Biblia & Coronâ,* vico vulgo dict. *Pater-Nofter-Row.* MDCCII.

ADVERTISEMENT.

WHereas for the Encouragement of this Undertaking, several Worthy Persons have Voluntarily been pleased to deposite each a *Guinea* to wards the Charge of these Plates, and others have promised to do the like or more asloon as this *First Decade* is published: This is therefore to satisfie such Curious Persons, that there are more *Tables* already done, and that the *Second Decade* will contain many things New and very Rare, which shall be published with all convenient Speed.

And for the Encouragement of such other Persons as shall advance 16 *Shil.* or a greater Summ, they shall immediately receive one half in what I have already published at the following Prizes, and the others as they come out.

	To Subscribers.	To others.
My 8 Centuries	0 2 6	0 3 6
Labells to *English* Plants above 400	0 2 0	0 3 0
Labells to *Officinal* Plants about 400	0 2 0	0 3 0
Gazophylac. Nat. & Artis *Dec.* 1.	0 4 0	0 5 0
The same mostly painted.	1 1 6	1 5 0
The *Catalogue* seperate.	0 0 6	0 1 0

Designing the Continuation of these Tables, as by several Friends I am earnestly desired, if therefore any Curious Persons, that are Lovers either of Art or Nature, will be pleased to communicate to me the things themselves, or their Designs of whatever is Curious under any Head mentioned in the Title Page of my GAZOPHYLACIUM NATURÆ & ARTIS, I will take care to insert them in my succeeding DECADES with a just Acknowledgment of them and the things they send, they please to direct them
For their *Humble Servant*
JAMES PETIVER

London

GAZOPHYLACII NATURÆ &c.

TAB. I.

1. **L**Acertus MARIANUS minor caudâ cæruleâ. *This is very particular in having a blew shining Tail, and is found about Trees in* MARYLAND, *from whence it was observed by my Curious Friend, Dr.* DAVID KRIEG M. D. & S. R. S.

2. Piscis *Quadrangularis* parvus, verrucosus & reticulatus. *Taken out of the Stomach of a Cod-fish, in an* East India *Voyage by Mr.* JAMES WHITE *Surgeon.*

3. Oscabrion CAROLINIANUS perelegans, squammis bifariàm variegatus. *This elegant Animal was given me by my Honoured Friend Dr.* MARTYN LISTER, *one of her Majesties* Principal *Physicians, to whom it was sent from* CAROLINA.

4. Asellus marinus, e nigro luteoque striatus. Sea-Hog-louse. *Brought up with Angling in* SMYRNA Bay, *and given me by Mr.* JOB MATHEWS *Apothecary.* an *Pediculus Marinus* Rond. *Pisc.* 576. Fig. L. 18. C. 28? an Poul de Mer *Rond.* Poiss. 412. Fig. L. 18. c. 26?

5. *Scarabœus* Hemisphæricus *Cochincelifer.* Cochinilla & *Coccinilla Offc.* Dale 539. 5. COCHINEAL. Act. Phil. 176. p. 1202. & No. 193. *It is here represented in its several states, that to the right being the Beetle, to the left the Chrysalis, and below as we have them in the Shops.*

6. <u>Plan-Orbis INDICA</u>, ex castaneo alboque striato, umbilico patulo. *This was brought from* Fort St. George, *to my Curious Friend* Dr. Grey.

7. Papilio Leucomelanus CANTABRIGIENSIS. *nobis.* Papilio *Leucomelanus* subtus viridescens marmoreus *Musf.* Petiver. 304. *Vernon's* half-Mourner. *I know not of any that hath met with this in* ENGLAND, *but Mr.* Vernon *about* Cambridge, *and there very rare.*

8. Papilio

8. Papilio ULISIPONENSIS ex nigro luteoque mixtus, maculis sanguineis aspersis. *This is eminently distinguish'd from others, in being sprinkled with some bloody Spots: It was observed about* Lisbon *by my Curious Friend* Mr. Jezreel Jones.

9. Xeranthemum speciosum e *CAP. BON. SP.* fl. albo maximo *Muf.* PETIVER. 500. After *GNAPHALOIDES* A. albo *Cap. B. Sp.* Breyn. *Cent.* 179. 2. Chryfocome f. Argyrocome Gnaphaloides *Africana* ampliffimis floribus Breyn. pr. 1. p. 27. 1 *an* Elychryfum *Africanum* lanuginofum latifolium, calyce floris argenteo & ampliffimo *Oldenl.* Inft. Rei Herb. 453. pl. 17. ? *I received this elegant Plant from* Dr. Frederick Ruych, *that accurate* Anatomift, *and Curious* Botanift *of* Amfterdam : *It being the only Specimen I have yet feen. It's diftinguifh'd from all others by its large white ftrawy Flowers and thick Cloath-like Leaves.*

10. Plantago MARIANA fpicâ prætenue *Muf.* PETIVER. 668. *This I had from* Dr. David Krieg , *who gathered it in* MARYLAND.

11. Ornitholgalum VIRGINIANUM luteum, foliis Gramineis hirfutis. *nobis.* Ornithogalum *luteum* parvum, foliis hirfutis D. BANISTER. *Ray H. Pl.* 1927. *This is pretty common in* CAROLINA, MARYLAND *and* VIRGINIA. *Its hairy Grafslike Leaves diftinguifh it from all I have yet feen.*

12. Gladiolus lacuftris VIRGINIANUS cæruleus, Sagittariæ folio. *nobis.* Sagittariæ *fimilis,* planta paluftris *Virginiana* fpicâ florum cæruleâ. D. BANISTER. H. Oxon. Sect. 15. p. 618. Tab. 4. Fig. 8. *I have received this from* MARY-LAND *and* VIRGINIA; *as alfo from* Mr. Edm. Bohun *who gathered it in* South Carolina, *where it Flowers in* June and July, *and is called by them* Wake-Robin.

13. Baccifera MARIANA, Clematis Daphnoidis minoris folio *Muf.* PETIVER. 363.

To the moft Reverend Father in God, THO-MAS *Lord* ARCHBISHOP *of* CANTER-BURY, Metropolitan *of* ENGLAND &c. *This* TABLE *is humbly dedicated by* JAMES PETIVER. *F. R. S.*

GAZOPHYLACII NATURÆ &c. TAB. II.

1. Capricornus NORWEGICUS nigrefcens, vaginis punctatis maculifque pallidis afperfis. *Mr. Richard Wheeler* fent me this from NORWAY.

2. Cantharus MARIANUS viridis pereIegans, vaginis fulcatis, fignaturis flavefcentibus ornatis. *This rare and elegant Infect was firft difcovered in* MARY-LAND *by the Reverend* Mr. Hugh Jones.

3. Papilio MARIANUS fufcus, areâ marginali oculatâ. *This alfo came from the fame Hand.*

4. Mufca AFRICANA flavefcens, caudâ trifetâ, alis nebulofis. *Mr. Richard Planer* caught this at *Cape Mount Serrado* near GUINEA.

5. Anagallis MARIANA lutea, foliis latis ftellatis. *This elegant Plant is diftinguifh'd by its broad Leaves, there being another fort which I have feen from thofe Parts with more, and much narrower.*

6. Schænanthus Avenaceus procumbens MADRASPA-TANUS *Beupleuri* facie *Muf. noft.* 577. *The heads of this Camels-hay are much fmaller and fhorter than any other Species I have yet feen, as are its* Leaves *and its* Sheaths.

7. Gramen Lagopoides GUINEENSE, fpica longa nutante *Mufei noftri* 238. *This* Grafs *hath* Spikes *upright as well as bending, particularly while they are young, as I have lately obferved in feveral Speciment Collected by* Mr. Watt *and* Mr. Skeen *Surgeons at* Cape 3 Puntas *on the Coaft of* Guinnea.

8. *Ilicis* foliis exiguis Frutex *Orientalis* Muf. noft. 250. *This* Shrub *has elegant fhining Leaves, I fhould be glad to fee it in* Flower *and* Fruit. Capt. Conway *brought it me from* Suratt.

9. Erica *Promont. Bonæ Spei* floribus albidis ftaminulis rubris *Muf. noftr.* 636. *This is known by its Cottony Heads with fhort red Stamina, and its fmooth Leaves diftinguifh it from* Muf. noft. 765.

10. Erica carnea *Promont. Bonæ Spei*, foliis & floribus villofis *Muf. Noft.* 637. *This has Cottony Heads like the laft, but they are commonly green and fometimes yellowifh as if mouldy, and from thefe Heads procced no ftamina as in the other.*

δ. 11. Papilio minor supernè fuscus, infernè viridis. *Observed by* Madam Glanvil *in the* West *of* ENGLAND, *as also by* Mr. Antrobus *about* CAMBRIDGE, *I have also once or twice seen it about* LONDON.

12. Scarabeus ALEPENSIS parvus villosus, vaginis e fusco aureoque mixtis. *Mr. Samuel Daniel Surgeon, caught this about* Aleppo.

To the Right Reverend Father *in* God HENRY Lord Bishop *of* LONDON *&c. this* Table *is humbly* Dedicated *by* JAMES PETIVER *F. R. S.*

GAZOPHYL. NATURÆ ET ARTIS.

TAB. III.

1. **L**ibella TURCICA major, alis *Locustæ. The sprinkled Clouds in the Wings of this* Adder-bolt, *are very dark, near to black.* Caught *about* Aleppo, *by* Mr. Sam. Daniel *Surgeon.*

2. Phalena MARIANA minor fulva, maculis nigris, albâ lineâ pulchrè aspersis. *This elegant Moth I first received from* Mary-land *and since from* Carolina.

3. Phalena MONSPELIACA alba minor speciosa, maculis sanguineis nigrisque aspersis. *This rare and beautiful Fly came among those Insects, which* Mr. Hen. Goff *and his Brother was pleased to give me,* Collected *in* India, *which the late worthy* Mr. Charlton *assured me he had long since caught about* Mompelier, *and upon comparing his with this, I find them the same.*

4. Papilio GUINEENSIS nigrescens, lituris albis asperiis. Mr. *Edward Barbar formerly sent me this from* Cape-Coast *in* Guinea. *The Ground of its Wings are black above and rusty below.*

5. Capricornus CAPENSIS niger, fasciis Aurantiacis.

6. Locusta CAPENSIS, alis inferioribus luteis. *This and the last were sent me from the* Cape of Good Hope, *with several other Insects very curiously preserved, by my ingenious friend* Mr. John Starrenburgh.

7. Erica

7. Erica CAPENSIS Coridis folio, flore rubello.

8. Tomineio MARIANA virefcens, gutture flammeo. The *Humming* Flame-Throat. *an* Guai-numbi 8. *Marcgr.* L. 5. c. 4. p. 197. 8? *Ray Ornith.* 167. 8. id. *Angl.* 232. 8. Tab. 42. Fig. 7. 9? *an* Oureffia five Tomineio *Cluf.* Exot. L. 5. c. 2. p. 96. Fig.? *The Reverend* Mr. Hugh Jones *fent me this beautiful Bird from* MARY-LAND.

9. Breyniana *Cineroides* CAPENSIS *nobis.* Frutex cineraceus mufcofus *Capitis Bonæ Spei.* Breyn. *Cent.* 24. c. 12. Fig. Tamarifci *feu* Myrica forté genus *Æthiopicum* Pluk. *Tab.* 297. Fig. 1. *Alm.* Bot. 159. pl. 13. *&* Tamarifci *feu* Myricæ forté genus *Æthiopicum,* muricato fructu intus tomentofo *Alm. Bot.* 361. pl. 11. *This, the next and* Fig. 7. Mr. John Starrenburgh *fent me with many other fair Specimens from the* Cape of Good Hope.

10. Hippuris *Coralloides* carnea, CAPENSIS, geniculis limofis.

11. Patella INDICA compreffa orificio magno ovali. *Mr. Charles Perry Surgeon* collected this in a Voyage to the *Eaft Indies.*

12. Patella compreffa, parva, exotica, orificio ftrictiori. *Given me by the Reverend* Mr. William Stoneftreet.

To Her Grace MARY, *Dutchefs Dowager of* BEAUFORT, *This* TABLE *is humbly Dedicated, by* JAMES PETIVER, *F. R. S.*

GAZOPHYLACII NATURÆ & ARTIS. TAB. IV.

Fig. 1. CIcada CAPENSIS variegata, marginibus tranf-parentibus. *Mr. John Starrenburgh* fent me this elegant Fly from the *Cape of Good Hope.*

2. Papilio MEXICANUS nigrefcens, lineâ lutefcente areâ miniaceâ notabili *Muf. noft.* 515. Caught at *La Vera Cruce* by *Mr. John Kirckwood* Surgeon.

3. Papilio MADRASPATANUS medius, flavedine & fufco mixtus, liturâ cæruleâ infignitus S. B. 5. 6. feu *Act.*

Phil. No. 276. p. 1023. 6. *This singular Butterfly* Mr. Edw. Bulkley *sent me from* Fort St. George.

4. Adiantum Philippense, folio rotundo laciniato. *Taken from a Design the Reverend Father* George Joseph Camel *sent* Mr. Ray *and me, from the* Philippine Isles.

5. Buccinulum album, lineâ sanguineâ spirale. *This singular and elegant Shell, the Reverend* Mr. Hugh Jones *gave me before his Departure to* Mary-land.

6. Stella CHINENSIS perelegans dupliciter radiata. S.B. 5. 1. seu *Act. Phil.* No. 276. p. 1023. 1. *Mr.* Samuel Brown *procured me this odd Animal from* China.

7. Capricornulus ORIENTALIS viridis guttulis nigris. *Given me by* Mr. Nich. Staphurst, *who found it on Ship-board in a Voyage from the* East Indies.

8. Umbilicus ORIENTALIS angustus serratus fuscus. *an* Unguis odoratus *CB in* Matth. 246. c. 8. Fig. ? Matth. in *Diosc.* edit. Valgris. A. D. 1560 p. 181. c. 8. Fig. ? Lonicer. in *Diosc.* p. 96. c. 7. Fig. Bizantia Pomet. pt. 2. p. 97. Fig. Ονυξ *Græc.* Achfar ateb *aut* Adfar althaib. *Arab.* i. e Unguis aromatica *Lat.* Ongle aromatique *Gal.* Narrow Conk-lid. *Mr* Charles Perry Surgeon brought me this only one I have yet seen from the *East Indies.*

9. Umbilicus latus fuscus. - *nobis.* Blatta Pomet. pt. 2. p. 97. Fig. bonâ. Blatta Bizantia *Offic.* Dale 549 4. Purpura Loniceri in *Diosc.* p. 96. c. 7. Fig, bon. Chesnut Oyster Muf. Reg. Soc. 141. Tab, 12. Fig. opt. Broad Conk-lid. Parkinson p. 1574. c. 14. *gives us Figures much resembling both these, and of this last* 2 or 3 *Varieties. I hope in time to receive these in their proper Shells, which will then enable me to give a better Account of both.*

10. Cochlea BENGALENSIS ore lacerato. *an* Cochlea compressa variegata, lateribus acutis, senis minimum dentibus donata List. H. C. L. 4. S. 5. Fig. 31. Tab. 577? *Mr.* Stocker found this Shell in the *Bay of* Bengale.

11 Fungus CAPENSIS subtus porosus. *This above resembles our* Rain-bow Mushrome, *but underneath is poune'd like a Thimble. My kind Friend* Mr. John Heardson *Apothecary, gathered this at the* Cape *of* Good Hope *in his Way to* Suratt.

12. Alga Spongioides MONSPESSULANA viridis. *Sent me from* Mompelier, *by that curious Physitian and Botanist* Dr. NISSOLE.

To the Right Honourable CHARLES Earl of
DORSET and MIDDLESEX, This TABLE
is humbly Dedicated by JAMES. PETIVER
F. R. S.

GAZOPHYLACII NATURÆ & ARTIS,

TAB. V.

Fig. 1. **C**Oncha Veneris parva undata, ventre maculato.
Concha Veneris parva, ventre subluteo macu-
loso, dorso undatis lineolis ex triplice ordine depicto List.
H. C. L. 4. S. 9. Tab. 661. Fig. 5. It's easily distinguish'd
from all others, by its peculiar Waves and spotted Belly.

2. Abrotanoides CAPENSIS Ericæ folio. This and
Fig. 4. Mr. John Starrenburgh sent me from the CAPE.

3. Echinus ovarius BARBADENSIS, radiis quinque ge-
minis venuste striatus Muf. Petiver. 124.

4. Breyniana CAPENSIS, capitulis albis plumosis. Were
it not for its plumose Heads this exactly resembles Fig. 9. Tab. 3.
of our GAZOPHYLACIUM.

5. Unicornu WIDENSE nodosum & verrucosum. an
Buccinum fuscum, nodosis striis distinctum List. H. C. L. 2.
Tab. 122. Fig. 18. Observed at WIDA on the Coast of Guin-
nea, by Mr. Wat Surgeon, and given me by Mr. Skeen.
Mr. John Kirckwood hath also found it at Old Calabar.

6. Linulum CAROLINIANUM humistratum Knawel
facie. This was brought me by my kind Friend Mr. Edm. Bohun
who observed it about Goose Creek in South CAROLINA.

7. Lewisanus CAPENSIS Serpilli folio. This differs
from No. 785. Musei nostri, in having its Leaves almost round,
like Mother of Thyme.

8. Onagra minima MADRASPATANA Pimpinellæ acu-
tiore folio. an Onagra Americana folio Betonicæ fructu his-
pido Inst. Rei Herb. 302. 6.

9. Folliculena seu Folliculum Phalena ovale, appendice
annulo terminante é MADRASPATAN S. B. 3. 11. seu
Act. Phil. No. 271. p. 860. 11. The Ring-Coffin. This and
the last Mr. Edw. Bulkley sent me from Fort St. George.

10. Xeran

10. Xeranthemum CAPENSE *Tartouraire* folio. *This altogether new and elegant Plant with the next,* Mr. John Starrenburgh *sent me from the* CAPE.

11. *Genista* tinctoria CAPENSIS, purpurea, foliis sericeis. *an* GENISTA *Africana* frutescens, foliis *Tartouraire,* fl. purpureo OLDENL. *Inst. R. H.* 644. 10 ?

12. *Stratiotes* quadrifolia *Lujula* facie. *an* Lemma *Theophrast.* Lugd. 1014. c. 11. Fig. *an* Lens palustris, altera *C B.* in *Matth.* 783. Fig. 2. *Lac.* Lugd. 1015. Fig ? *Lens* palustris quadrifolia *C B* Phyt. Fig. 7. 1. *I B.* V 3. l. 38. p. 777. Fig. *Chabr.* 566. Fig 3. *Park.* 1262. Fig. 2. Lente palustre *Durant.* app. Fig. *an* Lenticula palustris quadrifolia *C B.* 362. 4. palustris tetraphyllos *IB.* prodr. 115. 1. palustris 2. Tab. *an* Lenticulæ alterum genus *Cæsalp. This Specimen here Figured, I had from* WIDA *in* Guinea, *which having single Leaves only, best agrees with the* Lemma *Theoph.* Lugd. 1014. *From* Fort St. George *I have received what I take to be the same in Branches which very well agrees with the other Figure of* Lugd. p. 1015. *and the other Authors abovementioned, I have not as yet seen an* European *Specimen, by which I should be the better able to judge.*

To Sr. JOHN HOSKYNS Knt. *and* V. P. R. S. *this* TABLE *is humbly Dedicated by* JAM. PETIVER. F. R. S.

GAZOPHYLACII NATURÆ & ARTIS, TAB. VI.

Fig. 1. A*vis* MARY-LANDICA gutture luteo. *The* Mary-Land Yellow-Throat. *This and the next the Reverend* Mr. Hugh Jones *sent me from* MARY-LAND.

2. Randalia MARIANA procerior. *nobis.* Planta *Mariana* capitulis albis conglobatis *Muf.* PETIVER. 668. Mary-Land Randall-wort.

3. Cupressus CHUSANENSIS *Abietis* folio. *Mr. James Cuninghame Surgeon* sent me this with many other Curious Plants from CHUSAN an Island near LIAMPO in *China.* The *Leaves* are triangular, carinated, stiff, and stand off
from

from the Stalk, its Seed is brown and small, not much unlike *Buck-Wheat* but not so regular.

4. Conophoros CAPENSIS foliis parvis obtusis. *nobis. Abypum è Promont. Bonæ Spei* foliis minimis *Muf. Petiv.* 604.

5. Anguis *Exotica*, fusca, dorso albis maculis asperfis. *This elegant Snake I received from my worthy Friend Dr. Godfrey* Bidloo, Anatomick Professor *at* Leyden, *and Physician to his late Majesty King WILLIAM.*

6. Musca CAROLINIANA nigrescens, antennis magnis plumosis. *My kind Friend* Mr. Rob. Ellis *sent me this wonderful Fly from* Carolina.

7. Papilio CARTAGENIUS nigrescens, albâ lineâ prope extremitatibus alarum. Mr. *Richard Planer Surgeon* brought me this from *Carthagena* in *America.*

8. Concha Veneris *Emuyaca,* albida minor levis, circulo croceo S. B. 5. 35. seu *Act. Phil.* No. 276. p. 1028. 35. *where I have given you other Synonyms and its comparative Difference.*

9. Papilio ANGOLENSIS, *margine pulchrè oculata:* Mr. John Kirckwood Surgeon *was the first who discovered this elegant Fly at* Angola.

10. Balanus *Chinensis* aristatus *nobis.* an Balanus compressa & squammata *Muf. Regal. Soc.* 149. an Balanus *Rond.* aq. c. 29. p. 28. Fig ? Glans de Mer *Rond.* Gallic. c. 25. p. 21. Fig ? an Scaled Centre Shell *Muf. Regal.* Soc. Tab. 12. Fig. 6 ? *That most Curious Naturalist* Mr. James Cuninghame *first observed this at* Emuy *and since at* Chusan. *This seems very much to resemble the Figures in* Rondelet.

11. Jacea CAPENSIS Gnaphalii folio. an Jacea *Æthiopica* Stæchadis citrinæ majoribus tomentosa foliis, capitulorum spinis & squammulis ex aureo colore nitentibus *Alm. Bot.* 196. 6. Tab. 302. Fig. 3 ?

12. Papilio CAROLINIANA nigrescens maculis luteis. *My Kind Friend* Mr. Edmund Bohun *first observed this Butterfly in* CAROLINA.

To the Honourable Capt. CHARLES HATTON, *this* Table *is humbly dedicated by JAMES PETIVER F. R. S.*

GAZOPHYLACII NATURÆ & ARTIS, Tab. 7.

Fig. 1. GNaphalium CAPENSE spicatum, *Alyffi* foliis. *I am obliged to* Dr. Frederick Ruysch *Professor of Anatomy* and *Botany at Amsterdam for the discovery of this Plant.*

2. Pa-

2. Parietaria CANARIENSIS foliis ferratis fubtus lanu
ginofis. *This elegant Plant was firft obferved at the Canarie*
by my ingenious Friend Mr. James Cuninghame.

3. Argyrocome Capitis *Bonæ Spei* Thymi foliis *Muf.*
Petiver. 144.

4. Argyrocome *Virginiana* Atriplicis folio *nobis.* Conyza
Virginiana Halimi folio *Inft. Rei* Herb. 457. 7. Elychryfo
affinis *Virginiana* frutefcens foliis Chenopodii glaucis *Pluck.*
Tab. 27. Fig. 2. *Alm. Bot.* 134. pl. 12. Pfeudo-Helichryfum
Virginianum frutefcens Halimi latiori foliis glaucis *H. Ox.*
Sect. 7. p. 90. Tab. 10. Ser. 3. Fig. 2. No. 4. & Tab. 17.
Ser. 3. Fig. ult. Senecio *Virginianus* arborefcens *Par. Bat.*
225. Fig. & Defc. *Senecio* frutefcens *Virginiana* Atriplicis
folio *Ray* 1799. 14. *and* 1861. 6. *I have obferved this in*
Flower, *in the* Bifhop of LONDON *his moft* Curious Gar-
den *at* Fulham.

5. Papilio LUSITANICUS oculatus & marmoreatus.
The Portugal Grayling. *Caught about* Lisbon *by* Mr. Jezreel
Jones.

6. Folliculena CAROLINIANA e virgulis cooperta.
This Cafe-worm *as* Mr. Edward Bohun *calls it, he obferved*
many times in the Woods in Carolina *about* July; *Thefe are*
faftened to a fort of Willow *and guarded with little bits of*
Twigs like thofe I have obferved on the Phryganium *or* Caddus
in our Rivers.

A. 7. Phalena *Occidental. Angliæ* lituris ex aureo & argenteo mixtis.

A. 8. Phalena *Occident. Angliæ* alba, fignaturis nigris undatis. *This, the laft, and* Fig. 11. *all very rare, were firft dif-*
covered in the Weft *of* England *by* Madam Glanvil *a Perfon*
extremely curious in the Knowledge of Englifh *Infects.*

9. Tomineo CAPENSIS major, capite luteo. *This beau-*
tiful Bird I figured from a Painting my worthy Friend Dr. David Krieg F. R. S. *fent me from* Riga, *whilft it was befieged.*
Mr. John Rance Surgeon (*to whom I am obliged for feveral*
Shells *he brought me from* Borneo) *tells me he hath often obfer-*
ved this Bird at the Cape of Good Hope, *and that it hath*
a very long Tongue, which it throws into Flowers *as other* humming Birds.

10. Papilio CAROLINIANUS luteus, apicibus nigris.
I am extreamly obliged to that Generous Gentlewoman Madam
Williams, *who firft fent me this with feveral other very Curious*
Butterflies from Carolina. 11. Pha-

A. 11. Phalena *Occidental. Anglia,* virefcens, lineis obliquis albefcentibus. *This rare Moth with many others* Madam Glanvil *was pleafed to give me, who had obferved them in the* Weft *of* England.

12. Mufcus Ceranoides PALMENSIS comis digitatis, *Orchili* dictus *Muf. Petiver.* 436. *I take this to be the fame which* Theverus *fays grows in the* Canary Iflands *efpecially* Ferro, *on the Rocky Mountains where they call it* Oricelle *and the* Arabians Serth, with which they give a fine Dye to their *Spanifh Leather* Hift. *Lugd.* p. 175. lin. 13. Mr. James Cunighame *who gathered it at* Palma *one of the* Canary Ifles, *fays they call it there* Orchili, *and ufe it for Dying.*

To Dr. MARTIN LISTER *Her Majefties Phyfician and* F. R. S. *This* Table *is humbly dedicated by* JAMES PETIVER, F. R. S.

GAZOPHYLACII NATURÆ & ARTIS Tab. 8.

Fig. 1. **E**Upatoroides *Capenfis* capitatus. *Firft received from* Mr. John Starrenburgh.

2. Perficula guttulis croceis lineata. *an* Buccinum *Perficum* parvum, maculis rufis denfe depictum *Lift.* H. C. l. 4. *Sect.* 11. *Tab.* 803. *Fig.* 10.

3. *Concha Veneris* parva, fulva, circulis albis. *an* C. V. parva, ventre & lateribus albidis, dorfo fubflavo, albis majufculis & fphæricis diftincto *Lift.* H. C. l. 4. S. 9. *Tab.* 695. *Fig.* 42. Buff. Leopard *Cowry.*

4. Rhinoceros *Lufitan.* niger fplendens vaginis ftriatis. *an* Scarabeus Rhinoceros 3. *Aldr.* Infect. 451. Tab. 2. Fig. 3. *id.* Fr. 179. col. 1. Tab. p. 178. Fig. 3. *The Beetle Figured* on the Right Hand of the *Cervus volans* in *Imperatus* p. 694. feems very much to refemble this. *Mr. Jezreel Jones* caught it about *Lisbon.*

5. Capricornulus *Norwegicus* vaginis marmoreatis, antennis brevibus. *This and* Fig. 9. Mr. Richard Wheeler *fent from* Norway.

6. Scarabeus *Capenfis* pilofus vaginis rubris, plurimis punctulis albis afperfis. *This elegant Beetle* Mr. Starrenburgh *fent me amongft other* Cape Infects.

7. Phalena plumata permaxima *Orientalis* oculata *Muf. Petiver.* 729. *Goliah.* Mr. James Cuninghame *fent me this caught by* Mr. George Thurlow *in the* Straits *of* Sunda, *as* Mr. Hunter Surgeon fince his Return from *Chufan* informs me.
8. Ca-

8. Capricornus *Ruſſicus* cinereus, cornubus longiſſimis *Scarabeus* 7 ex Ruſſia *Moff.* 181. Fig. *id.* Angl. 1007. Fig. and 1008 *Deſcr.* Dr. Godfried Klem *one of the* Czar's *Phyſicians ſent me this from* Muſcow : *The ſame was alſo found by* Mr. Handley *a Neighbour in his own Garden here in* London.

9. Curculio *Norwegicus* niger, ſignaturis flaveſcentibus aſperſis.

10. *Perſicula* lineis croceis circundata. *an* Buccinum *Perſicum* parvum, faſciis rufis denſe depictum *Liſt.* H. C. l. 4. *Sect.* 11. *Tab.* 803. *Fig.* 9 ? *This has Lines inſtead of Specks, in which it differs from* Fig. 2. *above.*

11 *Cimex* ſuccinatus pedibus aliſque nigerrimis. *I am not certain from whence I received this, perhaps from the* Cape.

12. Filago *Capenſis* minor ſpicata. *This has the Face of our* Engliſh Cudweed *but much leſs.*

To Dr. Tancred Robinſon *Fellow of the Colledge of Phyſicians and Royal Society, this Table is humbly dedicated by* J. Petiver.

GAZOPHYLACII NATURÆ & ARTIS, Tab. 9.

Fig. 1. Teſtudinulus *Philippenſis* luteus, nigro maculatus. *The* Luzone *Turtle-Lady, I thus call it to diſtinguiſh it from* Fig. 3. *in the next* Table.

2. 3. Aurelia *&* Erucago Ejuſdem. *Theſe are after the Draughts the Reverend Father* George Joſeph Camel *lately ſent me from* Manilia.

4. Buccinulum dentatum *Mediterraneum*, ſtriis faſciatis maculatum. *an* Buccinum *dentatum* parvum, leviter ſtriatum variegatum ventrioſum *Liſt.* H. C. l. 4. Sect. 11. Tab. 823. Fig. 42?

5. Papilio *Angolenſis* ex pullo alboque mixtus. *Brought from* Angola *by* Mr. John Kirckwood *Surgeon.*

6. Alga *tubuloſa* albida navibus adhærens. *This I found plentifully growing to a* Ships *ſide in the* River Thames.

7. Concha *Veneris* minor, maculata & oculata. *nobis.* C. V. parva, latiuſcula, paululum gibboſa, ventre maculoſo dorſo, fuſco & albis innumeris & paucis nigris puncturis depicto *Liſt.* H. C. l. 4. S. 9. Tab. 696. Fig. 43.

8. Cato Simius volans *Cameli.* The Flying Cat-Monkey. *See its Deſcription in the* Philoſophical Tranſactions *No.* 277. p. 1065. 1. *This ſtrange Animal is found in the* Philippine Iſles, *and its uſual Abode there is on* Trees.

9. Ba.

9. *Balænas* compreſſus albus, ſex fiſſuris ſulcatus. *nobis.* Act. *Phil.* No. 255. p. 10. *This odd Shell Mr. James Cuninghame brought me among the reſt from the* Iſle *of* Aſcenſion.

10. Papilio albus *Angolenſis* apicibus miniaceis. Mr. John Kirckwood *firſt brought me this from* Angola, *it hath ſince been caught at* Wida, *by Mr.* Watt *and Mr.* Skeen *Surgeons.*

11. Papilio *Capenſis* flaveſcens verſicolor, apicibus nigreſcentibus. *This ſingular Fly Mr.* John Starrenburgh *ſent me from the* Cape of Good Hope, *the ground of its Wings are yellow, varying with a Philæmot Bluſh, if they hold it at a certain Poſition between you and the Light.*

12. Tipula *Londinenſis* anguſtiſſima. *This I have obſerved on ſome* Ponds *about* London : *It's much ſlenderer and leſs than the common* Water-Spider.

13. Tipula *Hamſtedienſis* brevior, ex croceo variegata. *I have as yet met with this only in ſome Ditches about* Bell-ſize *at* Hamſtead.

14. Alga verrucoſa *Capenſis. My Curious Friend Mr.* Starrenburgh *ſent me this with ſeveral other elegant* Sea-Productions, *which ſhall be figured in my next* Decade.

To Dr. HANS SLOAN, Fellow *of the* Colledge *of Phyſicians, Secretary of the* Royal Society *&c. This Plate is humbly Dedicated by* JAMES PETIVER F.R.S.

GAZOPHYLACII NATURÆ & ARTIS Tab. 10.

Fig. 1. **M**Elilotus *Suratenſis* minimus. Mr. John Heardſon, *was ſo kind to ſend me this amongſt other Plants which he collected about* Surat.

2. Hemiſphæricus *Luzonicus* luteus, nigro inſignitus. *Here are repreſented the different changes of this* Cow-Lady, *after the Deſigns which* Father Camelli *ſent me.*

3. Anguis *CAPENSIS* tricolor. *The Back of this is red, the Sides yellow, and the Spots black. I figured this from a Painting* Dr. David Krieg F. R. S. *ſent me from* Riga. *This Serpent with ſeveral other* Animals *I find amongſt ſome* CAPE Paintings, *which our worthy Kinſman* Dr. Sherard *hath lately given me to* Figure, *ſeveral of them I have already done in my next* Decade.

4. Scarabeus elaſticus major *Americanus*, capite bimaculato *Act. Phil.* No. 246. p. 396. 13. & *Scarabeus* colore griſeo, ſcapulis binis quaſi oculis nigris, mollitie pubeſcentibus notatus *Act. Phil.* No. 171. p. 812. 32. *The* Velvet-eyed

Virgi-

Virginia Snap-Beetle, *See its* Description *with* Mr. Bani-ster's Remarks and mine *in the Two aforesaid Places.*

5. Perficodes argentea, maculis nigris.

6. Papilio *Sulphureus*, lunulis cæruleis, nigris lituris in-fignitus. *This exactly resembles our* English Brimstone But-terfly *Muf. noft.* No. 1. *were it not for those black Spots, and apparent blue Moons in the lower Wings.* This is the only one I have yet feen.

7. Coccothrauftus *CAPENSIS* ruber, roftro hiante, è *Pi-Ɛturis* D. Krieg. *The* Cape-Cardinal. *This in Colour and Shape very much resembles the* Virginia Red-Bird *or* Nightingale, *in* Mr. Ray *of* Birds p. 245. Tab. 44. Fig. 2. *But what is peculiar to this is its* cleft Bill. *My Kind Freind* Mr. Rance Surgeon *tells me he hath frequently seen this Bird at the* Cape *where it's called the* CARDINAL.

Δ. 8. Buccinulum *fluviatile* heteroftrophon. *I have met with these in some* Ponds *and* Ditches *about* London.

9. Papilio *Surinamensis* caudatus minor, verruculis ex aureo argenteis, fubtus eleganter afperfis. *This very beau-tiful Butterfly with* Fig. 6. *my late worthy Friend* Mr. William Charlton *gave me to* Figure *a little before his* Death : *I have lately received it with* 3 *or* 4 *other* Surinam Flies, *which were altogether new to me, from* Dr. Frederick Ruyfch *Phy-fician and Botanift at* Amfterdam.

10. Mufcus Scoticus Corallio incruftatus. *Got in a fresh River near* Clacmannan *on* Forth *within a few Miles of* Stir-ling ; *procur'd me thence by my Curious and Worthy Friend* Mr. James Hamilton Surgeon *in* Edinburgh.

11. Planorbis minor fluviatilis acie acutâ. *Cochlea* fufca limbo circumfcripta *Lift.* H. C. l. 2. Tab. 138. Fig. 42. *Cochlea* fufca altera parte, planior & limbo infignita, 4 fpi-rarum L. A. *Angl.* Hift. p. 145. Fig. 27. *I have obferved this in the flow running* Waters *beyond* Weftminfter, *and in feveral little Rivers about* London.

12. Coralloides *Philippenfis* cærulea punɛtata. *Obferved in the* Philippine Ifles, *by that Curious Perfon* George Jofeph Camel, *who lately fent me a Draught of this, and I fuddenly ex-pect from him many other Rarities in Nature.*

To Mr. John Owen *this* Table *is humbly Dedicated by* James Petiver *F. R. S.*

FINIS.

GAZOPHYLACII
NATURÆ & ARTIS
DECAS SECUNDA:

In quâ **ANIMALIA, FOSSILIA, PLANTÆ,**
Omniaque Rariora **ARTE** producta

DESCRIPTIONIBUS brevib⁹,& **ICONIBUS** illuſtrantur.

A **JACOBO PETIVER**, Pharmacop. *LONDINENS.*
& **REGIÆ SOCIETATIS** Socio.

GAZOPHYLACII NATURÆ
& ARTIS, TAB XI.

FIG.1. *Lichen* MADRASPATANUS *Algoides*, marginibus verrucoſis.

    2. *Luffa* **MALABARICA** reticulata, fructu de-
corticato. *This is the peel'd or* decorticated *Fruit of
the* **PICINNA** Hort. Malabar. *Vol.* 8. *Tab.* 7. *pag.* 13. I
have given the *Synonyms* and *Vertues* of it in the *Philoſophical
Tranſactions,* N° 277. *p.* 1061. *pl.* 239. My worthy Friend
Mr. *Edward Bulkley*, Surgeon *at Fort St.* George, *procured me
this from* Perſia.

    3. *Cochlea* oblonga ſtriis flavicantibus nigris.

    4. *Nerita* **BARDADENSIS** inſtar *plumæ* eleganter macu-
lata. *This is a very beautiful* Shell, *and varies much in* Colour *and* Spots.

B   5. *Buccinu-*

5. *Buccinulum* MADARASPATAN. edentulum, è nigro alboque fasciatum.

6. *Plan-orbis* pulchre undata, ventre elato albido. *an* Trochilus planus subfuscus opere quodam vermiculato, ex toto depictus *List. Hist. Conchyl.* lib. 4. *Sect.* 8. *Tab.* 651. *Fig.* 48. Given me by my Curious Friend Dr. *Robert Gray.*

7. *Myrtus* GUINEENSIS *Epimespili* folio.

8. *Papilio* Luzonicus maximus nigrescens, maculis coccineis subtus perbelle notatus S. B. 6. 6. seu *Act. Philosoph.* N° 277. p. 1066. 6. where you may see it *described,* This is a large and very beautiful Insect, and is distinguisht from others by its deep *Scarlet spots* which in the *Figure* are exprest in *White.*

A. 9. *Papilio* minor fuscus, subtus striatus. *The Hair-Streak.* This being brown both above and below, perhaps differs only in Sex from Mr. *Rays* Purple-Streak *Mus. nostr.* 319. which is purple above and much paler than this beneath.

A. 10. *Papilio* minor fuscus, duplici lineâ inferne præditus, *The brown double Streak.* This and the last are very rare Flies, I first saw them in Mr. *Sam. Dales* Collection of *Insects.*

A. 11. *Papilio* minor fuscus, campo aureo, lineâ geminâ subtus ornatus. *an* Hoef. *Tab.* 12. *Fig.* 1. *The Golden brown double Streak.* This and the last may be *Male* and *Female.* Caught by my Neighbour Mr. *Benj. Harris, Aug.* 31. 1702. *in the Hest* near *Croydon.*

12. *Ornithopodium* MADRASPAT. *Bupleuri* folio. Mr. *Edw: Bulkley* sent me this with Fig. 1. and several other *Curious Plants,* with *Shells, Insects,* &c. from *Fort St. George.*

To His Grace HENRY Duke of BEAUFORT, This Table is humbly dedicated by JAMES PETIVER, F. R. S.

GAZOPHYLACII NATURÆ & ARTIS, TAB. XII.

FIG. 1. *Proscarabeoides* CAPENSIS, singulatis, pedibus plumosis. *This very odd Insect with* Fig. XI. *I copied from* Dr. *Sherard's Cape Paintings.* The *Legs, Head, Shoulder* and *Sides* are of a *Fleshy colour*, the *middle* of the *Back* yellow.

A. 2. *Testudinarius* HAMSTEDIENSIS tetramaculatus. *I never observed this but once, and that in* Cainwood *near* Hamstead.

3. *Tagetes* CHINENSIS *fol.* undulatis, *fl.* duplici, *rad.* Cordiali. *Herb.* nost. *Chin.* Tab. 27. Fig. 3. *This is that wonderful Plant which our Curious Friend* Mr. James Cuninghame *mentions in the* Philosophical Transactions Nº 280. pag. 102. *and says the* Chinese *value it from* Ten Tael *to one or two thousand a single Root according to its bigness* : Each *Tael* is reckoned at about 6 *s.* 8 *d.* *By drinking its* Infusion *for some time they assert it prolongs Life, and turns Grey Hairs into* Black. *An odd Tradition of its first Discovery is related in the aforesaid* Transactions, *to which I refer you.*

4. Auris INDICA non perforata.

5. Bombylus LUSITAN. è nigro cœrulescente. Mr. *Jezreel Jones* brought me this amongst many other Curious INSECTS which he had observed about *Lisbon*.

6. *Scarabeus* impennis rotundior CAPENSIS.

7. *Concha Veneris* parva, undata, apicibus purpureis bimaculata.

8. *Papilio* SURINAMENSIS ex aurantio nigro luteoque mixtus. *I first received this from* Dr. Ruysch, *and since from* Minheer Levinus Vincent, *two very curious Persons at* Amsterdam.

9. *Accipitrina* LIVORNICA perbelle striata. *I first received this from* Legorn, *since which my kind and worthy Friend* Mr. Jez. Jones *brought it me from* Lisbon, *he caught it flying about a Candle in* October 1698. its *Eyes*, whilst alive, are like *Rubies*. It frequents the *Jasmin Flowers*.

10. *Papilio* è fusco & albo eleganter mixto, à Promontorio Tricuspidato. *Caught at* Cape tres puntas *on the* Coast *of* Guinea *by* Mr. Skeen, Surgeon.

11. Aran-

11. Araneoides CAPENSIS fafciata, lutefcens, pedibus è nigro maculatis. *The Body whitifh, but the fwathes about it, and the Legs yellow, the laft fpotted with black.*

12. Grus CAPENSIS caudâ criftatâ. *The Bill of this beautiful Crane is partly yellow, his Creft and Eye-lids Red, that part of his Head above and below his Eyes blue, as are the edges of the Feathers on his Body, the reft White, the Feathers of his Tail, (if rightly painted) are alternatively Red and Blue.*

To *Mr.* ROBERT ANTROBUS *of* Peter-Houfe *in* CAMBRIDGE, *This Table is humbly Dedicated by* JAMES PETIVER, F. R. S.

GAZOPHYLACII NATURÆ & ARTIS, TAB. XIII.

FIG. 1. *Papilio* JAMAICENSIS è fufco lutefcente, fubtus virefcens croceo mixtus, *NOBIS.* Baker *Infect.* Tab. 1. Fig. 8. Dorf.

2. Scorpio JAVANICUS major pilofus, è nigro cærulefcente fplendens, *NOBIS.* Scorp. *Zeylanicus* niger maximus *Muf. Sibbald.* Sc. 116. Indicus niger, magnitudine Cancrum fluviatile æquans *Muf. Leyd.* 144. *id.* min. 56. Ghoniffa *Zeylon* : an S. è *Barbaria* Moff. 205. Fig. 204. & *append.* p. 330. ad cap. 10. *id.* A. 1049. an 'Sc. de *Tunifi* Muf. *Cofpian.*

The *accurate* Swammerdam *in his Curious Hiftory of Infects edit. Lat.* p. 147. Tab. 6. *gives a Figure of one fomewhat like this, but bigger, and feems particularly to differ in having but three joynts in the Tail, and ours five or fix as the leffer have.*

Bontius *in his* Hift. Natur. & Medic. *lib.* 5. *cap.* 4. *p.* 56. *feems to mention this, where he fays* Scorpiones quoque copiofos & grandes fert hæc *India* (i. e. *Java*) vidi enim qui partem quartam ulnæ implerent, coloris è nigro cyanei & fplendefcente, *which Shining and Colour this has.*

Mr. Charlton, *that late moft Curious Preferver of all Natural and Artificial Rarities, was pleafed to give me this amongft other Curiofities, fince which Mr.* Bulkley *hath fent me them from* Fort *St.* George, *and Mr.* Ed. Bartar *from the* Coaft of Guinea.

3. Scolopendra CAPENSIS major lutefcens, caudâ longiore.

4. Lichen

4. *Lichen* viridis foliis densè ftipatis, extremitatibus bifidis vel trifidis. *Obferved about* Tunbridge.

5. Scarabæus ALEPENSIS pilofus viridis, lineis albicantibus punctatis. *Brought me from* Scanderoon *by Mr.* Sam. Daniel, *Surgeon, who caught it* Apr. 28. 1690.

6. Scarabæus GALLICUS è nigro croceoque mixtus, f. *Cruciatus* minor. *This Dr.* David Kriegh *obferved about* Paris.

7. Locufta-Talpa CAPENSIS pedibus longis. *This comes next of Kind to our* Gryllo-Talpa, *or Mole Cricket, but its Feet are longer, and the Body partakes more of a naked Locuft, or large Grafhopper. Its painted with a mixture of Afh and Dark, or dirty Colour.*

8. Tellina MADRASPATANA fafciata & undata. *an* Tellina latior fafciata & undata quadam pictura confpicua *Lift*. H. C. l. 3. Tab. 378. Fig. 221.

A. 9. *Scarabeolus* niger noftras fupra aquam velociter circumnatans. *The Water-Flea.*

I obferve this very common all Summer in moft Ditches and graffie Ponds about London ; *it fwims on the furface of the water very fwiftly in quick turnings, and fomewhat circular motions, generally feveral together.*

10. Vefpa VIRGINIANA impennis ex nigro rubroque mixta *Act. Phil.* N° 271. p. 808. *This* winglefs Wafp *I have had from* Virginia, Maryland, *and* Carolina.

11. Cercopithecus LUZONIS minimus D. *Camel.* Magu vel Booot *Indorum.* This feeds on the *Prickly Pear,* and other Fruit, it rarely appears in the day time, whence its thought to be dim-fighted. When it fuckles its Young, it ties it to its Body, as expreft in the *Figure,* with the twigs of a twining Plant call'd *Pamago.*

12. Nerita JAMAICENSIS ex albo nigroque teffellatus. *an* Nerita profunde fulcatus ex albo nigroque variegatus paucis & exiguis dentibus ad columellam, ad roftrum multis & longa diductis *Lift.* H. C. l.4. S. 6. Tab. 597. Fig. 9. *This pretty Shell is frequent on the Shores of* Jamaica *and* Barbadoes.

To Mr. JACOB BOBART, *Botanick Profeffor of the Phyfick Garden in* Oxon, *This Table is humbly Dedicated by* JAMES PETIVER, F. R. S.

GAZO-

GAZOPHYLACII NATURÆ & ARTIS. TAB. XIV.

FIG. 1. Afplenium PHILIPPENSE, foliis aduncis, viminibus adnafcens. *Polypodium* falcatum *Cameli*. Bocalas *Indis*. This adheres to Trees by its hoary fibres, as our *Virginia Creeper* does to Walls by its tendrels.

A. 2. *Numifma* Inaugurale ANNÆ REGINÆ *Magna* Britanniæ.

A. 3. Phalena minor *noftras* fulva, alis limbo nigro infignitis. *I never but once obferved this Moth*, viz. *May* 3. 1696. *in a Broom-Field by Sir* William Hick's *Wood, beyond* Hackney Marfh.

A. 4. *Mufca* oblonga *noftras* nigra. *Found about Hedges in April and May*.

5. *Phalena* plumata MARIANA, caudata, virefcens, oculata *Muf*. PETIVER. 733. *I firft received this elegant Moth from* Maryland, *and have fince feen it from* Chufan. *The Reverend Dr*. Lewis *hath alfo fent it me from* Fort *St*. George.

A. 6. *Lichen* arboreus albefcens, fegmentis cornigeris, fubtus aterrimus. *This was firft fent me from* Norway. *I have fince obferved it about* Tunbridge *in two or three places*.

A. 7. *Cimex* niger noftras, albo maculatus. *an* Lift. in *Goed*. app. Tab. 5. *Scarab*. Angl. Fig. 8? *I have met with this in the Spring on funny Banks*.

8. Lacerta MARIANA undata, fubtus cœrulea. *This is a rough fcaled Lizard, with blackifh waved lifts on the Back, and blue on the Chin, and each fide of the Belly, fent me from* Maryland.

A. 9. *Papilio* oculis nigris, fubtus marmoreus *Muf*. PETIV. 307. The *Tunbridge* Grayling. *Very rare about* London.

10. *Trochus* fafciis verrucofis, è rubro albo nigroque alternatim perbelle diftinctus. *an* Trochus denratus ruber nigris puncturis feriatim diftinctus *Lift*. H. C. 1. 4. S. 8. Tab. 637. Fig. 25. *an* Cochlea *Pharaonia* Pifcatoribus *Maris Rubri* Muf. Cafpian : *Beian*. 141. Fig. magn. p. 222. 3. per *Microfcop*. auct. *an* Umbilicus varius *Rond*. aq. 104. c. 39. Fig. *id*. Gall. 70. c. 23. *Venus* Bugle.

A. 11. *Papilio* croceus, apicibus nigricantibus. *Papilio* 5. Moff. 100. Fig. Dor. & Lat. id. A. 968. *Jonft*. Infect.

p. 41.

p. 41. Tab. 6. Fig. 5. *an* Hoef. Tab.9. Fig. 6. *The Saffron Butterfly.* I have obferved this formerly, but 'tis uncommon, and rarely met with.

12. *Buceros* max. *Rhinocerotis* niger, BORNEACUS. an *Scarabeus* Buceros Naficornis 1. *Huang* Luzon. *Cameli.* This elegant large Beetle, Mr. *John Rance* Surgeon brought me from the *Ifland* of *Borneo.*

To Mr. CHARLES DU BOIS Treafurer of the EAST-INDIA Company, This Table is humbly dedicated by JAMES PETIVER, F. R. S.

GAZOPHYLACII NATURÆ & ARTIS, TAB. XV.

FIG. 1. Libella MARIANA media compreffa, corpore cœrulefcente, nubibus latis medio alarum. *This and the next the Reverend Mr.* Hugh Jones *fent me from* MARYLAND.

2. Libella MARIANA media, corpore flavefcente, trinubilata. *I take this, and the laft to be* Male *and* Female.

A. 3. *Byffus* aureus DERBIENSIS humifufus. *This elegant fort of* Mofs *my Hearty Friend,* Mr. James Ayrey, *found in the* Peak *of* Derby, *in a Lane joyning to the Field where the marvellous Stones are, about two Miles from* Eldenhole *on the way from thence to* Buxton-Wells.

A. 4. *Fungellus* gramineus NORTHAMTONIENSIS, Dr. Sloan *obferved this little Mufhroom fpringing from the Leaves of dead Grafs, about* September *laft, on* Shepherds-Hill *near* Althorp, *the Seat of the* Earl *of* Sunderland *in* Northamptonfhire.

5. *Concha Veneri* affinis, albus, medio annulofo. *Concha* utroque latere fe colligens exotica *Col.* Purp. c. 20. Fig. p. 30. *Concha* cujus medio velut annulus circumjicitur, *Lift.* H. C. l. 4. S. 9. Tab. 711. Fig. 64. *an* Bonan. 145. Fig. 249. f. p. 162. Fig. 339 ? *Common in* Jamaica & Barbadoes.

6. *Lacertus* GUINEENSIS major, verruculis nigris albifque venufte obfitis. *A harmlefs and very beautiful Lizard found in* Guinea *where they call it* Pompom : *This, with many other Curiofities, was prefented me by Mr.* Richard Planer *Surgeon.*

7. *Cicada* TURCICA media. Mr. *Sam. Daniel* Surgeon, obferved this in *Chio* and the Neighbouring Ifles, where they are common on Trees, and frequently finging.

8. Nirata

8. Nerita JAMAICENSIS alba, parva, ſtriis caſtaneis. *an* Nerita exiguus nigrolineus, ore ſubcroceo. *Liſt.* H. C. l. 4. S. 6. Tab. 605. Fig. 31 ? *This my Honoured Friend Dr.*Sloan *was pleaſed to give me with ſome other* Jamaica *Shells.*

9. *Papilio* CAROLIN. Aurantiacus, maculis albis, limbis & venis nigris, faſciàque ſingulari ala inferiori cinĉta. *The diſcovery of this elegant Fly is owing to Madam* Williams, *who caught it in her own Settlement in* Carolina.

A. 10. *Scolopendra* parva terreſtris tardipes, junĉturis bipedibus. *I obſerved this in* March 1696. *under Moſs in the ſhady places of my Lord* Wotton's *Grove in Belſiſe* Hamſtead.

11. Rhombus faſciis ex albo nigroque catenatis, *an* Rhombus cylindro pyramidali, lineis ex rufo alboque interjeĉtis circumſcriptus, clavicula paululum exerta *Liſt.* H. C. l. 4. ſ. 10. Tab. 763. Fig. 12 ?

12. *Papilio* LIVORNICUS ſupernè nigreſcens, inferne aureus, faſcia alba utrinque inſignitus. *The White* Legorn Admiral. Mr.*Robert Barklay,* Surgeon, brought me this firſt from *Legorn,* ſince which it was caught in *London* by Mr. *Bonavert.*

To Mr. RICHARD DYER, *Fellow of* ORIEL *College in* Oxon, *This Table is humbly Dedicated by* JAMES PETIVER, F. R. S.

GAZOPHYLACII NATURÆ & ARTIS, TAB.XVI.

FIG. 1. Radix VIZIAGAPATANA, fuſca, ſulcis rhomboidibus *Tello Molle* diĉta. Mr. *Edward Bulkley* ſent me this odd Root from *Viziagapatan.* It's ſaid to be good againſt the ſtinging of Serpents.

A. 2. Gemma *Turcica* in *Hæmatite* ſculpta. *This was brought from* Smyrna *and procured me by my kind Friend Mr.* Job Mathews. *It repreſents an Old Man reaping Corn.*

3. Unguis MADRASPAT. fuſcus, ſtriatus, ſubtus rubicundus. *This Figure ſhews the inſide which is of a bluſh red, the outſide is brown, and finely ſtriated.*

4. Tavaracare MALABAR. fl. albo, folio Nerii latiore, NOBIS. *Manga* fruĉtu venenato, oſſiculo cordiformi, nucleo gemino *Raii* H. Pl. 1552. c. 20. Odallam *Malab.* Uro *Bram.* Hört. *Mal.* V. 1. Tab. 39. p. 71. *Fl. Mal.* 192. 1. id. Fol. *I cannot believe with Dr.* Syen *the Commentator of this firſt Ver*
lumen

lumn, that this is the wild or Poyson Mango as he asserts; for had it that deadly quality the experienced Malabars *would have found it out, which they take no notice of.*

5. Tavaracare MADRASPAT. minor, cortice tenuiſſimo. *This is a smaller sort of* Coccus de Maldiva *found on the shores of Fort St.* George *and sent me thence by the Reverend Dr.* Lewis. *I take this to be the Fruit of the last Tree, the Description of it in the* Hort. Malab. *cited under Fig.* 4. *very much agreeing with it. I should be very glad if the Curious would send me a Branch of it,* in Leaf and Flower, with the Fruit on it.

A. 6. Stella HIBERNICA echinata. *Echinaster seu Stella coriacea pentadactyla echinata D.Lhwyd* ; an *Stella* pectinata *Rondel* aq. 120. c.12. *Fig.* 9. *This that Curious Naturalist Mr.* Edward Lhwyd *found near* Slego *in* Ireland, *as also at* Penſans *in* Cornwal.

7. Phalæna Chuſan. flava, (ſignaturis nigricantibus. *This singular Moth, with several other Insects, my Curious Friend Mr.* James Cunninghame *sent from* Chuſan *in* China.

8. Stellula HIBERNICA glabra. *Asteriscus ſ. Stella* pentadactyla exigua, Canis marini corio utrinque munita *E. Lhwyd. For this and several other elegant Species of* Sea Stars, *I am obliged to my Worthy Friend Mr.* Edw. Lhwyd *who found this at* Bondrouſe, *in the County of* Donegal *in* Ireland.

9. Chama MADRASPAT alba, undis caſtaneis. *This the Reverend Dr.* Lewis *sent me with several other Shells from Fort St.* George.

A. 10. Papilio *Fritillaricus* minor. *Muſ. noſt.* 324. *This hath been caught about* Cambridge, *but rare about* London.

A. 11. Phalæna CANENSIS nigreſcens, quatuor albis maculis aſperſa. *This elegant Moth I have caught in* Cane Wood *near* Hamſtead-Heath, *but very rarely.*

12. Anguis CAPENSIS argenteus maculatus. *He seems streak'd with blewish Silver,* along which *are many small spots. I copied it from a Painting Dr.* Sherard *was pleased to favour me with.*

To MAURICE EMMET, *Eſq; Fellow of the Royal Society, This Table is humbly Dedicated by* JAMES PETIVER, F.R.S.

GAZOPHYLACII NATURÆ & ARTIS, TAB. XVII.

FIG. 1. Retrochulus parvus *Italicus*. an *Cochlea* alba umbilicata, limbo acuto circumdata, claviculâ omnino planâ f. comprefsâ *Lift*. H. C. l. 1. Tab. 64. Fig. 62. *This is a small* Trochus *reverft, having its Head flat and Belly raifed, given me by Dr.* Sherard, *who found it about* Rome.

2. Phalena MARIANA argentea minima, nigris maculis afperfis.

3. Siliquaftrum RIGENSE *Limacis* cinerei facie *Muf. PETIVER.* 843. *This refembles our fmall Slug, and like it, is whitifh below, but brownifh above. It was found about* Riga.

4. Buccinulum PERSICUM olivare. an *Buccinum* 7 orbium leviter umbilicatum, mediis orbibus paululum tumidis *Lift*. H. C. l. 2. Tab. 108. Fig. 1. *This Dr.* Godfreid Klem *one of the* Czars *Phyfitians procured me from* Perfia.

5. *Simia-Sciurus* lanuginofus fufcus, ex JOANNÆ infula. an Cercopithecus *Indicus* Bugee *dictus* Raii *Synopf. Animal.* 358. *The Wool of this is brown, foft and curled like that of a Lamb, it has feveral properties of a* Squirrel, *fitting often upright when it eats, which generally is done by his* Incifores, *and reflecting his bufhy Tail. This ftrange Creature is now alive (viz. May* 1703.) *at Mr.* Dottins *a Drugfters in* New-gateftreet, *who had him about* 12 *months fince brought from* Joanna. *His Delineation was taken by that Celebrated Anatomift Mr.* William Cowper.

A. 6. *Cochleola* alba fafciata CANTABRIG. umbilico parvo. an *Cochlea* alba leviter umbilicata, pluribus fafciis circumdata, claviculâ productiore *Lift*. H. C. l. 1. Tab. 59. Fig. 56. *I obferved thefe on* New-Market-Heath *near* Cambridge.

7. Phalena MARIANA percruciata.

8. Phalena MARIANA fulvefcens cruciata. *This is a Kind of the laft, but the crofs here goes not to the edges of the Wings.*

A. 9. *Pectunculus* minimus lævis, intus argenteus, cardine ferratâ *Muf. Petiver* 845. Silver Cochle. *Found on our own Coafts.*

10. Taggee GUINEENSIBUS, *Radix* forte *Trafi* generis. *This feems to be a Root of a fort of* Cyperus, *has a thin Skin, and eats as pleafant as an* Almond : *Mr.* Rich. Roberts

gave

gave me some of these, who brought them from the Gold Coaft *in* Guinea.

11. Scarabeolus MARIAN. exiguus, vaginis lutefcentibus, ftriis nigris diftinctus. *Its Shoulders are yellower than the Sheath Wings, its Horns very fine, long, black, and joynted.*

12. *Phaletoides* Apiformis MARIAN. fplendore nigrefcent. argenteis maculis eleganter afperfis. *This fingular Infect, with the laft, and Fig. 2. the Reverend Mr.* Hugh Jones *fent me from* Maryland.

13. Filicula è *Gallipoli* villofa, Afplenii facie. an *Lonchitis* afpera Ilvenfis *Lugd.* 1221. Fig. *an* Lonchitis folio Ceterach *C. B.* 359. 3. *under which name he hath confounded four if not more Plants together. I am very much obliged to Mr.* Baker *at* Gallipoly *for this Plant, who fent it me by the Name of* Ceterac, *there being fome amongft it.*

To Dr. RICHARD RICHARDSON Phyfician at *North Bierly* in *Yorkfhire,* This Table is humbly dedicated by JAMES PETIVER. F. R. S.

GAZOPHYLACII NATURÆ & ARTIS, TAB. XVIII.

FIG. 1. *Buccinum* nigrefcens, maculis albis afperfis, ore gibbofo purpurafcente.

A. 2. Cochleola *fluviatilis,* gyris alte incifis. *I have obferved this in Frefh water, and if I miftake not, in the* New River.

3. *Phalena* maxima CHUSAN. obfcure fufca, marginibus eleganter undulatis. *This large and elegant Moth, altogether new, Mr.* James Cuninghame *fent from* Chufan.

4. *Tellina* parva radiata, intus omnino purpurafcens. *Thefe are pretty common in* Rock-work, *but I know not where they are found.*

A. 5. Buccinum CORNUBIENSE è Caftaneo & albo fafciatum. *Dells* Winckle : *He firft fending it me from the* Lands end. Mr. *Dandrige* hath alfo obferved it about *Deal* and *Dover.*

6. *Sidereon* five *Serpentaria* mirabilis montana *Kieg.* Phyt. *Curiof.* Fig. 213. Berg-Slangen Kruyd *Belg.* Munt. Herb. p. 751. cap. 330. *This very odd Plant is faid to grow on the Mountains of* Stiria *and* Hungary. *I fufpect this Figure is too much humored, and doubted whether there were fuch a Plant in*

Nature

Nature, until Dr. Sherard, *that most accurate Botanist told me he saw a Design of it done by that Laborious Naturalist* Conradus Gesner, *amongst the Figures of two Volums of Plants, being such he had observ'd growing about him. These are now in the Hands of Dr.* John George Volkamer, *Physician at* Nurenberg : *I shall be very much obliged to him or any other, who will be pleased to send me a Specimen of it.*

7. Cardamomum Luzonicum Coniforme *Ticala* dictum. *The Reverend* Father Cameli *sent over the Design of this elegant Plant. Its Description you may suddenly expect to see in the third Volume of Mr.* Ray's Universal History of Plants, *which is now in the Press.*

A. 8. *Cochleola* oblonga fluviatilis. an *Cochlea* parva subflava intra 5 spiras finita *List.* H. An. *Angl.* p. 135. Fig. 19. an *Cochlea* parva pellucida, operculo testaceo cochleatoque clausa *List.* H.C. l.2. Tab.132.Fig.32. *This is no bigger than a small Cherry-stone, oval, and not above half an Inch long, whereas Dr.* Lister *describes his to be as big as a Horse-Bean, and three or four Inches long. I find this in the* Thames *and* New-River.

A. 9. *Cylindrus* lapideus *Byerleus* compressior Echini facie, acetabulis majoribus oblongis, è puteis *Carbonariis,* R.Richardson. *That Curious Naturalist and Physician Dr.*Rich. Richardson *found this in the Coal Mines belonging to Mr.* Will. Pollard *near* North Byerly *in* Yorkshire.

A. 10. Papilio LINCOLNIENSIS Fritillaricus, fasciis subtus pallidis. The *Lincolnshire* Fritillary. *First observed there, and given me by Madam* Glanvile. *The Curious Mr.*Dandridge *hath lately caught him not far from* London.

A. 11. *Cylindrus* lapideus *Byerleus* compressior Echinitæ laticlavii maximi facie, acetabulis rotundis è puteis *Carbonariis* R. Richardson. *Observed in the same place with* Fig. 9.

12. Ostrea *Ulyssiponensis* minor rugosa. Mr.*Jezreel Jones* his *Lisbon* Oister. First observ'd by him on the shores near that City.

To the most Learned Dr. WILLIAM SHERARD, *Consul* SMYRNA, *This Table is humbly Dedicated by* JAMES PETIVER. F. R. S.

GAZOPHYLACII NATURÆ & ARTIS, TAB. XIX.

A. FIG. 1. Schiftus *Byerleus* impreffis reticulatis. *Taken from a Defign which Dr.* Richardfon *was pleafed to prefent, with feveral others, to Dr.* Sloan, *of fuch Foffils as he had obferved near his own Habitation at* North Byerly *in* Yorkſhire.

A. 2. *Scarabæus* arboreus major Caſtaneus. *The great Brown-Tree-Chaffer.* Goed.178. Tab.78. *Lift.* in *Goed.* 265.Fig. 111. *id.* app. Scarab. *Angl.* Tab.1.Fig.1. an *Scarabæus* arboreus *Moff.* 160. Fig.*id.* A. 1014. *Gr.* V. 1. p.9. Tab.4. an *Hoef.*Tab.16. Fig.12. an *Aldr.* Infeć. Tab. 5. Fig. 2. p. 453. *id* Fr. 178. Jonſt. *Infeć.* Tab. 14. *The Dorr or Hedge-Chaffer,* Muſ. Regal. Soc. 168. Very common all the *Summer.*

A. 3. Phalæna OCCIDENTAL. fulva, trifafciata. *Given me by* Madam Glanvil, *and is the only one I have yet feen.*

4. *Phalæna* fafciata perelegans, extremitatibus ſerratis. an *Goed.* 155. Tab. 67. *Lift.* in *Goed.* 81. Fig. 30. *id.* A. 38. The Furbeloe. *I firft caught this at Sir* Francis Leigh's *in* Kent. *Mr.* Antrobus *and Madam* Glanvile *have alfo fent it me.*

5. Sagittaria CHINENSIS foliis ternis longiſſimis *Herb.* noſt. *Chin.* Tab. 12. Fig.3. Sa heo chaw *Indigenis.*

6. *Ranunculus* globofus CHINENS. fl. pleno Aurantiaco. *Witung te boa.* Herb. noſt. Chin. Tab. 18. Fig.18. *This is a beautiful Plant, and would be a fine Ornament in our Gardens.*

7. Calceolus PHILIPPENS. pumila, Plantaginis folio rad. Alexipharmaca. *an* Katſula Kelengu *Malab.* Capura Catari *Bram.* Hort. Malab. V. XI. Tab. 41. p. 81. Dofa *aut* Dufu *Luzonenfibus*, in Samar & Leyte *Gozol.* Sinæ *Samlay* & in *Jucatan* Scabal chau i. e. *Reginam Plantarum* vocatur. *This Soveraign Plant I have figured from a Defign of the Reverend G.* Joſ. Camel, *formerly fent to Mr.* Ray *and me, which he fays grows in fhady moift places on the dewy Mountains of* Silan.

8.Arbor MANILENSIS Juglandis folio pentapetala, cortice Emetico. *Manonangtang* Indigenis *or Jail-deliverer,* aliis *Tambal* feu Medicina de *Carigara,* ubi abundat. *A Dram of the innermoft or third Bark of this Tree, is given in powder*

as

a very succesful Vomit in Fevers, ill Habits, and the Dropsie ; it also expels Poison, and brings away Worms. I received this from the same hand, with the last, it grows plentifully in many places of the Philippines.

9. Cylindrus MADRASPAT. medio nebuloso; clavicula carneâ. an *Rhombus* ventricosus, callosâ columellâ *List.* H. C. l. 4. S. 10. c. 3. Tab. 723. Fig. 10 ? *This and the two next the Reverend* Dr. George Lewis *sent me from Fort St.* George.

10. Buccinum MADRASPAT. nodosum, striis fasciatis.

11. Tellina MADRASPAT. triquetra, medio fasciata, extremitatibus tessulatis.

A. 12. Entrochus SEPTENTRIONAL. major compressus. *Dr.* R. Richardson *was pleased to send me this amongst many other uncommon Fossils.*

To the Reverend Mr. WILLIAM STONESTREET, This Table is humbly Dedicated by JAMES PETIVER. F. R. S.

GAZOPHYLACII NATURÆ & ARTIS, TAB. XX.

FIG. 1. Nodiflora MANILENSIS Onobrychidis folio, Rutæ odore. *Ruta* Luzon. *sylvestris Spicata* Camel.

2. Amomum verum *Encalada.* This is *figured* from a design which P. J. *Encalada* sent to *Father Camel,* from whom I had it. The *Cassemuniar* very much resembles it, which I have given a *Figure* of in my third *Decade.* Tab. 27.

3. Hemionitis *LUSON.* 1. s. H. minima vario & gratioso folio *Camel.* It sports variously in its Leaves, and grows about a Span high.

4. Trochus INDICUS è rubro & pallido radiatus, *Brought me by Mr.* John Stocker *from the Bay of* Bengale.

5. Macer veterum C. B. 408. Macer *Græcorum* Park. 1590. c. 36. Fig. p. 1688. Macer *Dioscorid.* & *Græcorum* J. B. l. 3. p. 262. Fig. *Chabr.* 18. Fig. 5. Macer arbor Antiquorum *Kiegl.* Phyt. Curios. Fig. 13. Macerboom der *Ouden Belg.* Munt. *Herb.* 88. Ulmo affinis, fructu vesiculis membranaceis & semine intus incluso composito *Rait* Hist.

Hift. Plant. 1779. c. 1. *This ftrange and much defir'd Tree,
the* Portuguefe *call* Arbore de las Camaras è Arbore Sancto
i.e. Arbor Dyfenteriæ & Arbor Sancta. The *Bramin Phyficians* call it *Macre,* and the *Malabars* Arbore de Sancto
Thomæ & Macruyren. *Avicen* fay's the *Arabians* call the
Bark of the Root *Talifafar,* and all the *Indian Phyficians* ufe
it with wonderful fuccefs in *Dyfenteries,* and other *Fluxes.*
It's faid to grow in divers parts of the *Eaft-Indies* : I hope
therefore it's not impoffible to procure *Specimens* of it in
Leaf and *Fruit.*

6. Pifcis *Brafilianus* cornutus. The *American* Toad-
Fifh. *Willughbeii* Hift. Pifcium p. 90. c.3. Tab.E.2. Fig.
1. Guaperva *Brafil.* Marcgr. 150. Fig. *Jonft.* Pifc. Tab. 36.
Fig. 6. p. 40. Defc. Pira Utoewah *Laet* Gall. 510. Fig.
The Brafil Toad-Fifh. *This is found on the fhores of Brafil,
and feveral other Coafts of the* Weft-Indies.

7. Bagre *Brafiliana,* corpore maculato. Bagre 2 Will.
Hift. Pifc. Tab. H.7. fine *defcr.* Bagre 4 *Jonft.* Pifc. Tab. 36.
Fig. 4. p.143. defc. *Bagre* alia fpecies f. ultima Marcgr.
174. Fig. & defc. Curui 1. *Pifon.* Ed. 2. p.63. Fig. *It's a
very wholefome Fifh, and found plentifully in St.* Francis *his River in* Brafile.

8. Carabus BENGALENSIS è cupreo virefcens. *Given
me by Mr.* John Stocker.

9. *Cochlea* inverfa, dentato ore. *Cochlea* variegata 7 dentibus donata fcilicet 2 in fundo oris & 5 ad labrum, claviculâ inverfâ *Lift.* H. C. l. 1. Tab. 99. Fig. 100. *Cochlea
turbine antico. The fore whirl'd Snail* Muf. Regal. Societ.
136. Tab. XI. Fig. 8. *Bonan.* p. 161. Fig. 330. & 1. The
Topfie Turvy Snail.

10. Cancer *Agathenfis* teftâ variegatâ. *Cancer* varius f.
marmoratus *Rondel.* Pifc. l. 18. c. 20. p. 566. *id.* Gall. 406.
Gefn. nom.aq.206. Fig. 3. s. ult. *id.* Hift. aq. 186. Fig. 1. *id.*
Fr. 158. Fig. 1. *Aldr.* An. ex. 200. c. 22. Fig. *id.* Br. 67.
Tab. 4. p. 66. Fig. 3. *Cancer* marmoratus f. varius *Jonft.*
An. ex. 22. Tab. 6. Fig. & Tab. 7. Fig. 13. *Rondelet's
Marble Crab, This he no where obferved but on the rocky fhores
of* Agde *in* Languedoc.

11. Cancer *Lerinæ Infula* chelis curtis fed cruribus longis.
cancer βϱαχυϗήλων *Rond.* 568. Fig. *id.* Gall. 407. c. 20. Fig.
Jonft. An. ex. 23. Tab. 6. Fig. 12. *Aldr.* An. ex. 205. Fig. 3.
id.

id. Fr. Tab. 4. p. 66. Fig. 16. *Gefn.* nom. aq. 207. Fig. 1. *id.* Hift. aq. 186. Fig. 2. *id.* Fr. 158. Fig. 2. The fhort Claw'd *Lerina* Crab. *This is rarely met with, but on St.* Honorat *an* Ifland *formerly call'd* Lerina *near* Antibes *in* Provence.

12. *Lacertus* fquamofus minor fetulis afperfis. an *Demon* Thebanicus junior ad fingulas fquamas pilis inftructus feu μαχαιρα γ❍ fquamatus *Thebanicus* Muf. Leyd. *Maf.* N° 295. *This intire Animal,* Madam Herman *fent me fome time fince from* Leyden.

To Dr. JOHN WOODWARD, M. D. *Phyfick Profeffor of* Grefham College, *and one of the College of Phyficians,* LONDON, *This Table is humbly dedicated by* JAMES PETIVER, F. R. S.

F I N I S.

GAZOPHYLACII
NATURÆ & ARTIS
DECAS TERTIA:

In quâ ANIMALIA, FOSSILIA, PLANTÆ,
Omniaque Rariora ARTE producta

DESCRIPTIONIBUS brevib9,& ICONIBUS illuftrantur.

A JACOBO PETIVER, Pharmacop. *LONDINENSI*,
& REGIÆ SOCIETATIS Socio.

GAZOPHYLACII NATURÆ
& ARTIS, TAB. XXI.

FIG. 1. Cathedra *Naturalis*, è Radice *Theæ* miıè contexta, ab Infula CHUSAN. This wonderful Elbow-Chair the *New Eaſt India Company* preſented to our late *Preſident* of the *Royal Society*, the *Lord Summers*, Baron of *Eveſham, &c.* who was pleaſed to add it to the Curioſities of that *Muſeum*. I have formerly ſeen a large *Root* of this very much matted, amongſt *Mr Charlton's* Rarities.

A. 2. *Schiſtus* BYERLEUS quadrangulariter impreſſus. Taken from a Deſign of Dr *Richardſon's*.

A. 3. *Cochinella* ANGLICA vulgatiſſima, ſeu rubra 7. nigris maculis notata. Hollar. Infect. Tab. 7. Fig. 8. *id*.

C
W

Wi. Tab. 3.Fig. xi. *Lift.* in Goedart. 268.Fig.112.id.Angl. 108. N. 112. Thefe are commonly met with moft part of the Summer.

A. 4. *Cochinella* ANGLICA bimaculata, s. minor rubra. Thefe are found with the laft, but more rare.

A. 5. *Cochinella* OCCIDENTALIS oblonga, rubra, tetramaculata. Madam *Glanvile* gave me this, and it's the only one I have yet feen.

6. *Cochlea* JAMAICENSIS depreffa bidens. *Cochlea* bidens ex parte tantum : columella margine obtufiore clavicula compreffâ *Lift.* Hift. *Conchylior.* lib. 1. *Tab.* 8:. *Fig.* 87. an *Lift.* Hift. Animal. *Angl.* append. p. 45. Tab. 3. *Fig.* 1, 2.? *This was given me by* Mr J. Savage, *who had it from* Jamaica.

A. 7. *Squilla* lacuftris minima, dorfe natante. *Obferved in the Spring, by* Mr Baker, Apothecary, *in the Ponds on the Common between* K. Henry's Walks *and* Kings-land. *I have hatched thefe from their Eggs.*

8 *Phafeolus* MADRASPATANUS femine compreffo nigro alboque eleganter ftriato. an *Chabr.* Icon. 140. Fig. 2. I. B. V. 2 l. 17. p. 267.

9. *Phafeolus* MADRASPATAN. minimus, Reniformis Bezoardicus. This and the laft 2 very beautiful Kidney-beans Mr *Edward Bulkley* fent me from *Fort St George.*

10 *The* Thea Shrub *is here* Figured *with its* Leaf, Flower *and* Fruit, *to accompany the* Root *above at* Fig. 1. *I have given the various Synonyms of this in the* Philofophical Tranfactions, N. 286. p. 1428. 92.

11. *Patella* BORNEOCA auriculata tenuis. *This odd Skell* Mr J Rance, Surgeon, *brought me from the Ifland* Borneo.

12. *Stockerus* BENGALENSIS viridis nigro maculatus. *This is a new Genus of the* Beetle kind, *the* Vagina *not being fplit but intire, from under which it expands its membranaceous wings, as the* Figure *expreffes, which is its* Flying pofture. Mr John Stocker, *my Curious Friend, being the firft that fhewed me this Species, I have chofe to diftinguifh it from other kinds by his name.*

To JOHN *Lord* SUMMERS, *Baron of* EVESHAM, &c. *This Table is humbly dedicated by* JAMES PETIVER, F. R. S.

GA.

GAZOPHYLACII NATURÆ & ARTIS, TAB. XXII.

FIG. 1. *Fructus* VIZIAGAPATAN, globofus, hexa-gonus, cortice fufco. *Prauna Rakha kria* Viziaga-patan. *Good in violent Fevers, and takes away the blackneſs of the Tongue.* Mr Edward Bulkley. *This is covered with a thin brown Shell, which peel'd off diſcovers a ſmooth Fruit equal-ly divided into 6 partitions, each of theſe has a thick woody incloſure, containing in the center a* Ricinus *like* Seed, *lying in a large* interſepimentum *or Bed.*

A. 2. Lyra *Harvicenſis*, pinnâ dorſali longiſſimâ, macu-lis cærulefcentibus. *Taken about* Harwich, *and preſented to the* Repoſitory *of the* Royal Society *by* Mr Bull, *Fiſh-monger.*

3. *Zerumbet* Officinarum *Dale* Pharmac. p. 366. 9. Fa-ther *Camel* (from whom I had this accurate defign) cal-led this *Zerumbeth,* and others the *Red* Ginger *of Ternate,* by the *Indians* Pangafam and Banglay. The *Malabar* Wild Ginger, Hort. *Malab*. Vol. xi. Tab. 13. p. 27. and that of *Zeylon,* which is accurately defcribed and Figured by *Dr Harman* in his Hort. *Lugd. Bat.* p. 637. who makes it the *Zerumbet* of *Garcias,* l. 1. c. 43. feem to be the fame Plant with this, or very near of kin. See a large *Defcrip-tion* of this, with its many *Uſes,* great *Vertues,* &c. in the *Appendix* to Mr *Ray's* 3d Volume of *Plants.*

A. 4. *Scarabæus* minor Filicinus. an Lift. *Hift.* An. *Angl.* app. Tab. 4. Fig. 3. Bracken-Clocks. *So call'd in the* North, *becauſe found on the* Brake, *or* Female Fern, *on which I have often obſerved them.*

A. 5. *Curculio* miniatus minimus. *I found this at* Ep-fom *the laft Spring, in company with* Dr Lifter *and* Dr Brey-nius, *Mr* Middleton Maffey *has obſerved it in* December.

A. 6. *Scarabæus* agreftis oviparus, Melanocyaneus fuc-co fanguineo, *The Bloody Egg Beetle.* I have obferved thefe of feveral fizes, and when taken they fpew out a bloody Liquor. *Lift.* H. A. A. ap. Tab. 4. Fig. 14.

7. Mr Fox *his* Bengale Bettle. *Its body green, the round ſpots yellow, and the others red with a yellowiſh border.* Muf. noft. 906.

8. *Papilio* IND. ORIENTAL. fufcus, margine cœru-leo, fubtus Marmoreus. *This Elegant* Butterfly *I received in* Mr G..ff's Collection *of Inſects.*

9. *Scara-*

9. *Scarabæus* pectinatus minor villofus. *The hoary Chaf-fer.* Lift. H. A. A. *app.* Tab. 4. fig. 2. an *Mof.* 160· fig. 3. *id.* A. 1014. an *Hoef.* Tab. 1· fig. xi. This is hoary, and much lefs than *Gaz.* noft. Tab. 19. Fig. 2. and is rarely met with.

10, *Trochylus* MONSPESSULANUS exiguus, fafciatus, pyramidalis, *Lift.* Hift. *Conchyl.* L. 1. Tab. 61. Fig. 58. *Lift.* H. A. A. p 45. Tab. 3, Fig. 12. *This elegant Shell is pretty frequent about* Mompelier, *as* Dr Lifter *has ob-ferved.*

11. *Buccinum* BARBADENSE perelegans fafciatum. *Buccinum* 7 orbium fafciis fere bicoloribus, interdum tri-coloribus Iridis inftar depictum *Lift.* H. C. I. 1. Tab. 15. Fig. 10, an *Bonan.* 121. Fig. 66. *Our Worthy Friend* Dr Martin Lifter *was pleafed to give me this beautiful Shell with the laft,* April the 3d, 1697.

12. *Schiftus* BYERLEUS Caucaloides. *Thefe Ovals feem rough, like the Seed of* Caucalis *or* Baftard Parfly. *This, with feveral other impreft Slates, I received from my Worthy Friend* Dr Richard Richardfon.

To Dr HANS PETER CHARRIERE, M.D. This *Table* is humbly dedicated by JAMES PETIVER, F. R. S.

GAZOPHYLACII NATURÆ & ARTIS, TAB. XXIII.

FIG. 1. *Zedoaria* Officinarum. *This the* Indians *call* Damogcanfi. *It very much refembles the* Gaidoar, *or* Gedwar and Turmerick, *but is diftinguifht chiefly in its Leaves, this having a brownifh ftreak along the midft of each, which the others have not.* Ray *Syllab.* Camell. 23: 9.

2. *Porus Spongioides* Americana. *Here are 2 varieties of this, which perhaps may be the fame, the firft or bifurcated flat one is* Purplifh, *both externally and in the middle, and many of its pores are deeply made, the other is roundifh, pale without except the fpots, which are blackifh, and rarely perforated, the inner pith like the laft is purplifh. Both given me by* Mr Ro-binfon, Apothecary *in* Shandois-ftreet, *near* Covent-gar-den.

A. 3.

A. 3. *Scarabæus* triceros, niger, antennis pectinatis. *an* Bonceros *vel* Tauroceros *Moff.* 152. fig. 2. *id.* Angl. 1008. *Mr Dandridge* obferved thefe on *Hampftead-heath* in the Spring.

A. 4. *Scarabæus* fpadiceus, cornibus ferratis pediculis nigris. *an* Lift. H. A. A. *app.* Tab. 4. Fig. 5.? Obferved by *Mr Richard Middleton Maffey,* a very Curious Perfon in Natural Philofophy, about *Midfummer* in the *Phyfick garden* at *Oxon :* I have alfo met with it about *London,* but not common.

5. *Avicula* CHINENSIS è cærulea, alba & nigricante mixta. *Its Belly, Wing-fhoulders, Collar, and about the Eyes white, the reft blue ftrip'd with black ; Back, Breaft and Head blue. This the* Chinefe *paint in their* Pictures, Skreens, &c.

6. *Spongia* BARBADENSIS alba, Corallii facie. *This is perforated, fome few large enough to contain a Cherry-ftone, in which I have found fmall Shells, and therefore I conceive made by them for their receptacles ; the reft which it's full of, are but pin-holes, it may be blown through in any part, as you can through thin Cloath.* Mr Will, Stratton *brought me this, with fome Shells,* &c. *from* Barbadoes.

A. 7. *Capricornulus* NORWEGICUS fcaber, coftis nebulofis. *I firft received this from* Norway, *fince which* Mr Dandridge *hath obferved it on* Box hill *in* May. *an* Lift. H. A. A. *app.* Tab. 4. Fig. 8.

8. Papilio *Alpinus,* &c. Muf. Petiver. 502. *Mr Ray's* Alpine Butterflie. *The 3 Clouds next the body, and the 4 Spots in the under-wings are deep yellow, the Eye-fpots fometimes reddifh, the reft white and black.*

9. *Mus* araneus CAPENSIS maximus. *Taken from a Painting of* Dr Sherard's, *now* Conful *of* Smyrna.

A. 10. *Scarabæus* Viarius niger vaginis fulcatis. *I met with 3 or 4 of thefe* ☿ April 24. 1696 *in the Path way between* Bromly *and* London, *and the year before nigh* Cain-Wood.

11. *Scarabæus* Carnivorus niger, vaginis fulcatis ac rugofis. *This is fomewhat lefs than the Laft, both Shoulders and Sheaths are rugged : I found them* May the 3d, 1696. *in the intrails of* Poie-cats *and* Weafils *on* Sir William Hickes Common *near* Hackney.

12. *Scarabæus* pectinarius viridis, elytris quafi fractis. *The Rofe Chaffer.* an *Smaragdus* vel Viridulus *Moff.* 158 ?

id. A. 1013? *Merr.* pin. 201. 4? an *Scarabæus* viridis *Aldr.*
Infect. *ed.* Francof. p. 179. A. Tab. Fig. 6. T. 1. p. 178.
id. ed. Bon. 150. Fig. 6. an *Amst.* Infect. 6. p. 71. Tab. 13.
Fig. 6, 'f. 1. an *Scarabæus* Rutilus minor *Charlton* Exercit.
47. 4.? *Thefe are often found amongst* Rofes *in* June *and* July.

To Mr DIXON COLBY, Mafter of Arts of *Merton College*
in OXON. This *Table* is humbly dedicated by JAMES
PETIVER, F. R. S.

GAZOPHYLACII NATURÆ & ARTIS. TAB. XXIV.

FIG. 1. *Champacca* PHILIPPENS. flore ac fructu
ftellato. *Alanguilang* Zebuanorum. *Burac, Layo, Ha-
ramao Byfaiarum, In y an hua* Sinarum. *See* Father Camel's
Defcription of it in the Appendix to Mr Rays 3d Volume *of*
Plants, *pag.* 83. 2.

A. 2. *Papilio* Oculatus è fufco aureo mixtus, umbrâ
purpurafcente. *Mr Dale*'s Purple Eye. *This I obferved amongst*
Mr Dale's *Collection of* Englifh Butterflies, *and is the only
one I have yet feen.*

A. 3. *Papilio* Oculatus è fufco & flavefcente mixtus.
The Enfield *Eye.* Becaufe I have obferved feveral of them
on that *Chace*, I have feen them elfewhere, but not common.

A. 4. *Curculio* major fubcinereus undatus. *Mr Dandridg*
gave me this large Beetle, who obferved it in the *Spring*
about *Greenwich* and *Woolwich* in the Sand-holes of thofe
Pits.

5. *Pectunculus* lunulatus AMERICANUS fafciis alte
elatis. *an* Pectunculus *Maculatus, fafciis rarioribus, exafpera-
tus* Lift. H. C. L. 3. S. 4. Tab. 277. Fig. 114? *This Shell
has 6 or 8 high raifed fafciæ, which take their beginning from
the Heart-fide, but are not fo elevated on the other.*

6. *Capricornus* AMERIC. &c. Muf. Petiver. 708. *The
Campeachy Goat Chaffer.* The Sheaths of this elegant Beetle are white finely ftreakt with gold and black, as if Ja-
pann'd.

A. 7. *Scarabæus* impennis tardipes. *The flow legg'd Beetle.*
Moff. 139. Fig. *id.* Angl. 999. *I meet with thefe in* Cellars
and

and old Houfes, *it walks as if frozen, by which, and its ha-ving no membranaceous wings, it's eafily known from all others.*

8. Ninzin & Genfing *Officinarum* Dale *Pharm.* 340. 11. *Ray* H. Pl. 1338. *Pluk.* 101. 7. This is copied from a Painting now in the *Mufæum* of the *Royal Society,* the *Root* is efteemed as a great Cordial and Reftorative. It grows in *Japan* and *China.*

9. *Ranunculus* SICULUS fol. rotundo vix ferrato. *Ray* V. 3. app. 248. R. 4. Dr John Philip Breynius *gave me a Sample of this which he gathered in the* Phyfick-garden *at* Am-fterdam, *and I have figur'd it from a Defign by his own hand.*

10. *Nafcornis* Tauroceros MARIANUS, fplendens, Ca-ftanei coloris *Terra Mariana* Hift. *noft.* Natural. *feu* A&. Philofoph. N. 271. p. 814 45. Jones Mary-land Bull Rhinoceros. *This is of the* Comb-horn'd (*i. e. antennis pecti-natis*) kind, and is very fhining above.

11. *Capricornus* niger CAPENSIS fulcatus,6 albis macu-lis infignitus. *A very elegant* Cape Beetle *fent me from thence by Mr* J-Starembergh, *he hath alfo fent me another without fpots.*

12. *Sphondylus* BARBADENSIS parvus, altè fulcatus. *This my kind Friend* Mr James Ayrey *gave me, who had it from* Barbadoes; *it oft varies in its fhape, the tips of its hinges are always brown.*

To the Reverend Dr JOHN COVELL, Mafter of *Chrifts College* in CAMBRIDGE, This *Table* is humbly dedi-cated by JAMES PETIVER, F.R. S.

GAZOPHYLACII NATURÆ & ARTIS, TAB. XXV.

A. FIG. 1. *Phalæna* alba parva OCCIDENTALIS, fig-naturis marginibufque nigris. *This pretty Moth* Mad. Glanvile *firft fent me from the* Weft of England, *which* Mr John Perkins, Apothecary, *caught fince, in my company, on the high Chalky Mountains near* Rigate in Surry, ☿ July 1703.

A. 2. *Ichneumon* minor, zonis obfcuris. *This, the next, and* Fig. 10. *I find in the Spring on feveral banks about* London.

A. 3. *Ichneumon* minor niger, zonis luteis. *This is known from* Fig. 10. *in having that part below the narrow waft black, with 2 fmall yellow girdles parted in the middle.*

4. Re-

4. *Raniunculus* PARISIENSIS pumilus, Plantaginellæ folio *Hort.* noft. *fice.* Ray *Vol.* 3. app. 248. R. 3. *I am obliged to* Monfieur Vaillant, *Secretary to* Dr Fagon, *Chief Phyfician to* the King of France, *for the difcovery of this Plant, who obferved it about* Paris.

5. *Rana* CAROLINIANA maxima, voce Taurino. *The* American *Bull-Frog.* This is that great Frog *Mr Clayton* mentions in the *Philofoph. Tranfactions* N. 210. p. 125. and which the *Baron Labontan* in his Defcription of *North America,* p. 242. calls *Lowing Frogs.*

6. *Jacea* CAPENSIS fol. parvo hirto. capite vifcofo *Hort.* noft. *Siec.* Ray V. 3. app. 245. L. 2. C. 63. *Given me by* Dr Breynius, *Son to that Famous Botanift* Jacobus Breynius *of* Dantzick.

7. *Conophorus* CAPENSIS Pini folio *Hort.* noft. *fice.* Ray V. 3. app. 243. C. 63. *This Rare Plant* Mr James Cuninghame *brought me from the* Cape of Good Hope.

8. *Tellina* affinis JAMAIC. lunulata, cuneo productiore. *This my old Friend* Mr Patrick Rattry *brought me amongft a parcel of other Shells from* Jamaica.

9. *Pectunculus* AMERICANUS cordatus, fafciis craffis. *Thefe* fafciæ *or Circles are thicker fet, and nothing near fo high raifed as* Tab. 24. Fig. 5. *which with this came from fome part of the* Weft Indies, *I believe from* Jamaica or Barbadoes.

A. 10. *Ichneumon* minor, croceus, zonis luteis. *This comes next* Fig. 3. *but has an Orange lift below the waft, inftead of a black field.*

11. *Capricornus* CAROLINIANUS fufcus pallido afperfus. *This fingular Beetle* Mr Edmund Bohun *brought me from* Carolina.

12. *Phalæna* OCCIDENTALIS coloribus & alis undatis. *Glanviles tipt Furbeloe.* She being the firft perfon I receiv'd it from who obferved it.

To the Honourable JOHN EVELYN, Efq; F. R. S. &c. This *Table* is humbly dedicated by JAMES PETIVER, F. R. S.

GAZOPHYLACII NATURÆ & ARTIS, TAB. XXVI.

FIG. 1. *Onobrychis* MADRASPAT. Nummulariæ folio, Barbareæ filiquis *Hort.* ficc. *Petiver.* Ray *Vol.* 3. append. p. 247. O. 12. *This is faid to pod in* March. 2. *E-*

2. *Euonymus* CAPENSIS fpinofa *Hort.* noft. *ficc.* Ray V. 3. *app.* 244. E. 33. *Euonymo* adfinis *Æthiopica* fpinofa, *Lycii* foliis & aculeis, *fructu Euonymi* Pannonicæ *Clufii* grandiore *Almag.* Botan. *Tab.* 280. fig. 5. pag. 139.

3. *Phalæna* PHILIPPENSIS cinerea, maculis flavis, corpore zonis fanguineis intermixtis. *Papilio* polymitus omnium pulcherrimus *Camel.* Fig. 26. *Infector.* Mfs.

4. *Onobrychis* MADRASPAT. Nummulariæ folio, Ornithopodii filiquis *Hort.* noft. *ficc.* Ray V. 3. app. 247. O. 13. *This differs very little from* Fig. 1. *but in its pods, which are ripe in* June.

5. *Araneus* LUZON. Bovinus. *From the likeness of its Horns, ftanding almoft ftrait.*

6. *Araneus* LUZON. teftaceus trilunatus. *This is mixt with yellow and black.*

7. *Araneus* LUZON. cruftaceus, cornu lunulato. *Mixt like the laft.*

8. *Araneus* LUZON. teftaceus anguftus trilunatus. *This is not only narrower than* Fig. 6. *but the fpots tho of the fame colour, are differently plac'd:* *Thefe* 4 *were copied from Defigns the Learned* Father Camel *fent me.*

9. *Scarabæus* PHILIPPENSIS prafino-aureus, maculis luteo-albicantibus. *Cantharis* Luzon. Cetonia Prafino-aurea *Camel.* Mfs. *The belly is of the fame colour, but not ftriped.*

10. *Solea* PHILIPPENSIS argentea. *This is a flat edible Fifh full of Scales, it's* 2 *inches broad and a fpan and half long, Silvery above and brown below.*

11. *Scarabæus* MARIANUS minor fulvus, maculis nigricantibus afperfis *Act. Phil.* N. 246. p. 396. 9. *This the Reverend* Mr Hugh Jones *fent me with feveral other Beetles, &c. from* Maryland, *which I have given an account of in the aforefaid* Tranfactions.

12. *Ranunculus* aquaticus Plantaginis folio anguftiffimo *Inftit. Rei Herbar.* 292. pl. 12. *Hift. de Plantes* de Paris 525. *defcript.* opt. *This Plant* Monf. Vaillant *fent me the laft year from* Paris, *where it grows wild, and flowers in* July *and* Auguft.

To Mr PETER GELSTHORP, Mafter of the Society of *Apothecaries,* This *Table* is humbly Dedicated by JAMES PETIVER, F. R. S.

GAZO-

GAZOPHYLACII NATURÆ & ARTIS, TAB. XXVII

FIG. 1. *Caffamunier* Officinarum *Ray* V. 3. app. 243. c. 21. The defign of this Plant was fent me from *Mr Edward Bulkley* at *Fort St George* : This perhaps may be the fame with *Father Camell's* Zerumbet *Tab.* 22. Fig. 3. which I hope in time I fhall be able to determine.

2. *Olivaris* ftriata & fafciata. *an* Cochlea *alba* ventricofa bidens ftriis eminentibus exafperata *Lift.* H. C. l. 4. S. 5. c. 7. *Tab.* 588. *Fig.* 47. This in length and thickneſs rather refembles *Dr Lifter's* Fig. 49. but if it does, his twirls are much broader than ours, and feems fewer of them.

3. *Capricornulus* nigrefcens MARIANUS, undis & circulis flavefcentibus ftriatus. *Act. Phil.* No 246. p. 397. 20. The *Maryland* Waſp Beetle.

4. *Erica* HIBERNICA fol. Myrti pilofis fubtus incanis *Hort.* roft. ſicc. 244. E. 20. *Erica* S. Dabeoci D. *Lhwyd* Ray *Dend.* V. 3. p. 98. 30. Erica *Cantabrica* Flore maximo, foliis Myrti fubtus incanis *Inftit. Rei Herb.* 603. 5. Elem. Botan. 475. I had a fpecimen of this elegant Plant from my generous Friend *Mr Edward Lhwyd*, Keeper of the *Muſeum Aſhmoleanum*, who gathered it in *Ireland* in the places *Mr Ray* mentions.

5. *Papilio* PHILIPPENSIS cæruleus, maculis fubtus rotundis & triangularibus.

6. *Papilio* PHILIPPENS. oculis 7 oblongis fimbriatus. *I am highly obliged to the* Reverend Father Camell *for thefe 2 laft Infects, with many others, and their defigns.*

7. *Scarabæus* oblongus niger VIRGINIANUS, vaginis fulcatis, dorfo plano nitente. *Act. Phil.* 246. p. 396. 12. *Marfhal's* Virginia *Chaffer.*

8. *Scarabæus* MARIANUS viridis Rhinoceratos *Act. Phil.* N. 246. p. 395. 7. *The* Maryland *green Horn-Chaffer,* This is diftinguifht from the next in having horns.

9. *Scarabæus* MARIANUS viridis aceratos *Act. Phil.* No 246. p. 396. 8. *The Green* Maryland *Chaffer.* Both thefe are very common in *Maryland* and *Carolina.*

10. *Scarabæus* LUZONENS. elafticus, vaginis ftriatis. *Dango* Philippenfibus. *Tou have both fides of this Snap-Beetle figured from the Defigns* Father Camell *fent me.*

11. *Rhom-*

11. *Rhombus* albus fasciis flavis & mæandris alternatim perbelle depictus. *an* Rhombus *Lift.* H. C. l. 4. S. 10. c. 5. Tab. 786. Fig. 35. *This elegant Shell my Worthy Friend* Mr Charlton *was pleased formerly to give me.*

12. *Alga* PHILIPPENSIS carnosa edulis *Goso* dicta. *This Specimen I have* Figured *from a Sample the Reverend Fa-ther* Camell *sent me, it's transparent, yellowish, and of the consistence of* Gum Tragacanth. *Ray Syllab.* Camel. pag. 42. 12.

To Mr THOMAS GREENHILL, Chirurgeon, This
 Table is humbly Dedicated by JAMES PETIVER,
 F. R. S.

GAZOPHYLACII NATURÆ & ARTIS, Tab. XXVIII.

FIG. 1. *Papilio* SURINAMENSIS maximus, subtus per-belle oculatus ac marmoreatus. *This very large and beautiful Butterflie* Myn Heer Levinus Vincent *sent me, a-mongst several others, from* Amsterdam : *I find it also amongst* Madam Merian's *Figures* of her *History* of Surinam *Insects.*

A. 2. *Phalæna* Sulphurea, nebulis rufescentibus. *First observed in* Mr *Tillman Bobart*'s Collection ; *I have since seen it about* London, *but not common.*

3. *Scarabæus* pectinatus LUZON. aureo-smaragdinus.

4. *Rhombus* INDIÆ ORIENTALIS, spatiolis, catenis, fasciisque flavis, cætera albus, an *Rhombus* subluteus cy-lindro pyramidali, lineis quibusdam punctatis & fasciis undatis depictus *Lift.* H. C. l. 4. S. 10. Tab. 780. Fig. 27.

5. *Capricornus* LUZON. ex atro & aureo mixtus. *This elegant Beetle, with* Fig. 3. *the Reverend* Father Camell *sent me Designs of.*

6. *Avis* PHILIPPENSIS galeâ planâ. *Calao* Luzonen-fibus. *See an accurate description of this wonderful Bird by* Fa-ther Camell *in the* Philosoph. Transact. N. 285. p. 1394. 17. *Who tells me the Body is less, and the Tail larger than the Figure which he sent me represents.*

7. *Papilio* LUZON. è fusco & luteo superne mixtus. *This and the 2 next from the same hand with the last.*

8. *Pha-*

8. *Phalæna* LUZON. è fufco &albo utraq; parte confpicue commaculatus.

9. *Papilio* LUZON. luteus marginibus atris.

A. 10. *Trochites* perelegans Pyrite impreffus. *Dr Richardfon*, that Curious Obferver, fent me this elegant impreffion in a Copperas Stone from *North Byerly* in *Torkfbire*.

11. *Mantis* MEDITERRAN. rufefcens media. *Caught in the Straights by* M· Sam. Daniel *Surgeon.*

12. *Operculum* IND'Æ ORIENTALIS fuperficie verrucofo. *Firft given me by* Mr Charlton, *I have fince had it from the* Eaft Indies.

To the Reverend Dr HENRY JAMES, Mafter of *Queens College* in CAMBRIDGE. This *Table* is humbly Dedicated by JAMES PETIVER, F. R. S.

GAZOPHYLACII NATURÆ & ARTIS, TAB. XXIX.

FIG. 1. *Eryngium* fortè MAURITANICUM, fpinofum folio anguftiffimo *Hort.* noft. *ficc.* Ray V. 3. app. 244. E. 26. *an* Bupleurum *Hifpanicum* fruticofum aculeatum Gramineo folio *El. Botan.* 260. *Inft.* Rei Herbar. 310. 16. Signior Paul Boccone *now* Sylvius *had this from the Coaft of* Barbary, *and gave it to* Dr Sherard, *from whofe Specimen I defigned it. It's a very odd fhrubby Plant, and has fomewhat the face of a* Corruda ; *each Joynt is commonly armed with three woody ftrong Thorns, the largeft in the middle ; thefe ftand alternately, like the* Bambu, *on a crofs bended ftock ; from the bofom of thefe Spines comes 2 or 3 lefs, with as many long narrow Leaves of the ftiffnefs of* Holly ; *on the edges are many little protuberances, like the firft Leaves of* Epiphyllanthus *Jamaicenfis.*

2. *Euceros* LUZON. naficornis maximus *Bagang* dictus Camel. Mfs. de *Scarab.* Philippenfibus.

3. *Phalæna* GUINEENSIS flava perelegans & pulchre oculata. *This beautiful Infect my Hearty and Kind Friend* Mr Rich. Planer *brought me with feveral others from the* Guinea Coaft.

4. *Araneus* LUZON. mortiferus Smaragdino-aureus *Banayau* 1. Camel. Mfs. *Aran. Luzon.* an *Araneus* aureus *Niremberg* Hift. Nat. 291. c. 24. *an* Lavalava *Hernand.* Infect. Hift. p. 75. c. 28.

The Sting of this, if not cured by Fire or a Decoction of Dauva, *kills Man and Beast, these delight in the* Sambach Arabum, *or* Syringa, *and dwell in their twisted Leaves.*

A. 5. *Scarabeolus* SEPTENTR. vaginis aureis eleganter ftriatis, capite nigro: *This with* Fig. 8. & 9. Madam Glanville *sent me from the West of* England, *where she had observ'd them.*

6. *Araneus* LUZON. ex argenteo, flavo & fusco pulchre mixto, pedibus nigris.

7. *Astacus* LUZON. cornutus echinatus, albo, luteo & cinnabarino elegantissime variegatus. *Banagan* Philippensibus. *Camel. Mss. Piscium, Mollusc. & Crustac. Philipp.* The *design* he sent me is as big again as this *Figure.*

A. 8. *Testudinarius* aureus guttulis nigris asperfis. I once obferv'd this in a Meadow near *Woolwich.*

A. 9. *Scarabeolus* oblongus aureus maculis 13 in vaginis ornatus. *This something resembles our common* Lady-cow, *but is slenderer, and has 6 spots on each Wing, with one on the Fissure, as the other has but three.*

10. *Araneus* LUZON. torosus pilofus, totus fuscus: *The* Defigns *of this,* Fig. 4. & 6. *were sent me from that curious Observer of Nature,* Father George Joseph Camel.

11. *Cæcilia* BORN. &c. *Mus. nost.* 106. The ftrip'd Snake of *Borneo: This feems to be a familiar House-Snake, for my worthy Friend* Mr Silvanus Landon *caught him drinking in a Punch-bowl, after a sudden return with some Friends from it, in the* Ifland Borneo.

12. *Araneus* LUZON. gibbofus fubfufcus, per totum dorfum protrafto, elevato & flavo *Camel Mfs:* Araneor. *Philippensium.* Thefe lay whitifh Eggs in yellow filken globular Baggs.

To Mr EDWARD LHWYD, Keeper of the *Ashmolean Museum* in OXON. This *Table* is humbly Dedicated by JAMES PETIVER, F. R. S.

GAZOPHYLACII NATURÆ & ARTIS, TAB. XXX.

FIG. 1. *Pectunculus &c.* Mufcovitica *Mus. nost.* 728. Klem's Ruffia Mufcle. *It was first difcovered by that Phyfician, and is an elegant Shell.*

2. Hir-

2. *Hirundo* LUZON. venenata ruberrima Bangol, di&a. *This wonderful Fifh is red throughout : All its Flefh will in one Night by hanging up diffolve into a florid red liquor, which they ufe in ftaining, and is very lafting. It's a fpan and a half long, and hath Warts inftead of Scales.*

3. *Concha Veneris* cæruleſcens parva, utroque capite bimaculata, ventre late ferrato. *an* C. V. *Lift.* L. 4. S. 9. **Tab.** 624. Fig. 20. ? *This is always bluifh, but varies in its fpots and waves.*

A. 4. *Capricornulus* HAMPSTED. ſtramineus, ſignaturis nigris. *This fometimes varies in its magnitude, as in the Figures, but is always bigger than the next, and more rarely met with : Caught in Bear-wood beyond Hampſtead Heath.*

A. 5. *Capricornulus* HAMPSTED. exiguus, vaginis rubent. apice nigro. *I have obſerved thefe about* Midſummer, *on the Flowers of* Sphondylium *or* Cow Parſnip. *To whofe Umbells divers Infects refort.*

6. *Olivaris* BARBADENSIS vix dentatus, ex albo & Caſtaneo reticulatus, clavicula cærulefcente *an* Lift. H.C. L. 4. S. xi. Tab. 827. fig. 49. b. *Barbadoes* Net-Olive. *Thefe are diftinguifht from others by their blue tips.*

A. 7. *Buccinulum* oblongum Avenaceum. *an* Buccinum exiguum 5 anfractuum, mucrone acuto *Lift.* H. A. A. p. 122. Fig. 7. *Thefe I found at the Roots of old Trees in the* Lord Wooton's Grove *at* Hamſtead , *March* 7. A. D. 1697.

8. Lapis CHINENSIS Mayz referens. The *Mayz Stone.* Mr Will. Maple, *at* Apothecary's Hall, *was pleas'd to give me this elegant Stone ; it very much refembles the grains of* Turky-wheat *or* Mayz, *but thefe are alternately fet, and not one directly over the other.*

9. *Concha Veneris* cæruleſcens parva, utroque capite bimiculata, ventre feffile plano *an* C. V. *Lift.* H. L. C. 4. S. 9. Tab. 624. Fig. 21. ? *This is very like Fig. 3. but differs in having its Belly fmooth, and the Mouth only tooth'd.*

10. *Crotalaria* MADRASPAT. Pilofelæ folio *Hort.* noft. Sicc. Ray V. 3. app. 244. C. 194. *This and the next I lately receiv'd from my worthy Friend* Mr Edward Buikly *at* Fort St George, *as I had formerly done from* Mr Samuel Brown.

11. *Lens* MADRASPATAN. Elatines folio *Hort.* noft. Sicc. Ray V. 3. append. 246. L. 8. *The* Flowers are yellow, *lonely and with Stalks, each coming from the bofom of its Leaf, and are fucceeded by a fmall flat Lentile-like pod.*

12. *Argyrocome* CAPENS. fol. incanis lobati·. *Chryfocome* flore albo, foliis fubrotundis auriculatis *Capitis Bonæ fpei.* Breynij *Prodr.* 2do p. 33.3. D⸰ Breynius, *Son of this cele-brated Author, was pleas'd to prefent me with this fpecimen.*

To M⸰ JOHN THORPE, Mafter of *Arts* of *Univerfity College* in OXON. This Table is humbly Dedicated by JAMES PETIVER, F. R. S.

Tractatus varii, ad *Hiftoriam Naturalem* & *Medicinam* per-tinentes, prout extant à me editi in *Actis Philofophicis,* Anglice *vulgo vocatis* The Philofophical Tranfactions : *und cum eorum abbreviationibus.*

1. PLantæ quædam ex GUINEA, relatio *Nominum* nec non & *Virtutum* Act. Philof. No 232. pag. 677. *Ab-breviat.* Guin. *vel* Mat. Med. Guin.

2. Quædam *Synonyma* adjectitia, primo Volumini *Horti Medici Amftelodam.* Act. Phil. No

3. *Obfervationes Naturales* à *Boftone* in NOVA ANGLIA D. *Miffæ à Benjamin Bullivant* Pharmacopœo Act. Phil. No 240. p. 167. *Abbr.* Bull.

4. *Defcriptio* quarundam *Plantarum* ex UNANEER-COONDO Regione non ita procul à Fortalitio D⸰ *Georgii* in *India Orientali.* Act. Phil. No 244. p. 313. *Abbr.* Un⸰

5. *Relatio* quorundam *Animalium Plantarumque* MARI-LAND. miffa per *Reverend. D. Hugonem Jones.* Act. Phil. N. 246. p. 393. *Abbr.* H. Mar.

6. Defcriptio & Figura *Amomi legitimi.* Act. Phil. No 248. p. 2.

7. Tractatulus de *Faba S. Ignatii* unà cum *Icone* fua, Miffæ à Reverendo Patre *Georg. Jofepho Camello,* Jefuita. Act. Phil. No p.

8. *Tentamina* quædam ad probandum *Herbas* ejufdem *Claffu* five *Formæ* (magnam partem) eafdem fortiri *Virtutes,* in Differtatione habita coram *Societat. Regal.* Londin. Act. Phil. No 255. p. 289.

9. Catalogus *Conchyliorum* &c. collectorum in *Infula Af-cenfionis* per Curiofum Chirurgum D. *Jac. Cunninghame,* Act. Phil. No 255. p. 295. *Abbr.* Afcenf.

10. *Plantæ* MADRASPATANÆ fimul & earündem re-latio, Collectæ per D. *Samuel Brown,* Chirurgum, *Botaniftam* imprimis *Curiofum.* Act. Phil. No 264. p. 531. *Abbr.* S. B. Vol. *l.* 1. S. B. 1.

11. Bre-

11. Brevis relatio *Floræ Norimbergensis* in lucem editæ per *D. Volkamer* M·D· A&. Phil· No 265· p· 651·

12. Volumen Secundum *Plantarum* ex MADERASPA-TAN ab Eodem. *A&. Phil.* No 267· p· 699· *Abbr.* S.B.2.

13. *Animadverfiones* in Obfervationes *Infctarum* VIRGI-NIANARUM à *Jo. Banifter* A&. Phil· No 270· p· 807· *Abbr.* Ban· Infe&. Virg.

14. Liber Tertius *Plantarum* MADERASPAT· adje&is infuper aliquammultis *Animalibus* ex his oris, cum defcripti-onibus. *A&. Phil.* No 271· R· p· 843· *Abbr.* S· B· 3.

15. *Conchylia* quædam ex *Infula* MOLUCCA defcripta, quibus adjicitur *Quartus Liber* D· Sam· Brown *de Plantis* Indicis. *A&. Phil.* No 274· p· 927· *Abbr.* S· B· 4.

16. Ejufdem *Quintus Liber* de eodem : unà cum nonnullis *Animalibus* miffæ à pluribus *Regionibus* Indiarum· *A&. Phil.* No 276· p·1007· *Abbr.* S· B· 5.

17. *Defcriptio* quorundam *Animalium*, quæ à Rev· Patre *Camell* accepi ab *Infulis Philippenfibus* : quibus præmitti-tur *Liber 6.* D· Sa· Brown *Plantarum Officinalium* & aliarum *Medicinalium* ex INDIA *Curiofarum* A&. Phil· No 277· p· 1055· *Abbr.* S· B· 6.

18. *Volumen* Graminum *Indicorum* ex eodem : adjiciun-tur, *Conchylia* quædam à Rev· D· *Georgio Lewis*, *A&. Phil.* No 282· p· 1251· *Abbr.* S· B· 7.

19. Tra&atus *de Avibus Philippenfibus* à G· Jof· Camello *communicatus* A&.Phil· No 285· p·1394 *Abbr.* Cam·Av·Phil·

20. *Corallia* quædam aliaque *Submarina*, miffa ab *Infulis Philippenfibus* , nec non *Defcriptio* plurimarum *Plantarum* nafcentium in *Infula* CHUSAN prope *Chinam*, colle&arum à D· *Jac· Cnningham* S· Reg· S· *A&. Phil* No 286· p· 1419· *Abbr.* Chuf.

21. *Plantæ* quædam MADRASPATANÆ mihi miffæ à D· *Edwardo Bulkley* Chirurgo *admodum* Curiofo & *ab aliis* in 7 Libris præcedentibus non memoratis. *A&. Phil·* No 287· p· 1450· *Abbr.* E· B· Vol· 1· vel S· B· 8.

22. De *Ambaro* s. *Ambragrifea* à Rev· Camello *communi-cata*. A&. Phil· No 290· p· 1591·

23. *Dete&iones* quædam de *Cortice Peruviano* in Literis me datis a D· *Doctore Gulielmo Oliverio* M· D· & S· R· S· *A&· Phil·* No 290· p· 1596·

LONDON, Printed for *Sam· Smith* and C· *Bateman*, Bookfellers· 1704.

GAZOPHYLACII
NATURÆ & ARTIS
DECAS QUARTA:

In quâ ANIMALIA, FOSSILIA, PLANTÆ,
Omniaque Rariora ARTE producta

DESCRIPTIONIBUS brevib9,& ICONIBUS illuſtrantur.

AJACOBO PETIVER, Pharmacop. *LONDINENSI*,
& REGIÆ SOCIETATIS Socio.

GAZOPHYLACII NATURÆ
& ARTIS, TAB. XXXI.

FIG. 1. *Calao* avis roſtrum rubrum, galeatum, caſ-
ſide latâ. *Under this Title, the Curious and Learned
Father Kamel ſent me this Deſign with his Manuſcript
of* Philippine Birds, *now Printed in the* Philoſophical Tranſactions, N. 285.

A. 2. *Cantharis* azureus perelegans· *I firſt receiv'd this
in* Mr Darby *his* Collection *of* Inſects *formerly gave me, and
have ſince obſerved it about Houſes·*

A. 3. Scarabæolus *aureus*, capite nigro·

A. 4. Scarabæolus *aureus*, capite lineiſq; nigris·

A. 5. Planorbis *hortenſis* minima pulchre ſtriata· *Cochlea*
terreſtris compreſſa maculata & leviter ſtriata *Liſt. Hiſt.*

D   *Con·*

Conchyl. app. Tab. 4. *Our Curious Brother* Mr Sam. Dale *first diſcovered this and ſent it me. I have ſince obſerved it about* London.

6. Inhame MADRASPATAN. foliis binis pulchrè venoſis *Hort. noſt. Sicc.* 11. 19. ſeu *Ray* Hiſt. Plant *Vol.* 3. append. 246. *I am obliged to Mr* Edward Bulkley *for this Beautiful Plant, whoſe Leaves are the moſt elegantly veined I ever yet ſaw.*

A. 7. Scarabæolus niger, lateribus apicibuſque vaginarum aureis. *Found floating in a Ditch in* Biſhops Wood *beyond* Hampſtead Heath.

8. Coralloides epiſpongioſa PHILIPPENSIS, virgulis dilu·è purpureis, minoribus punctis. *Philipp.* Submar *Catal.* 14. ſeu *Act. Phil.* N 286. p. 1421. 14.

9. Pectunculus Venereus. *Pectunculus* ruber faſciis acutis & ex altera parte muricatis exaſperatus *Liſt.* H. C. Lib. 3. Sect. 1. cap. 3. Tab. 307. Fig. 146. *Olearij* Muſ. p. 62. 4. Tab. 29. Fig. 4.

10. *Echinus* perexiguus. *Echinus* omnium minima. *Aldrovand.* Teſt. 412. fig. id. edit. *Francof.* Tab. 10. fig. 23. p. 136. *I take this to be an* Indigena *on our Coaſt, finding them amongſt a parcel of Shells, which I believe are* Engliſh.

11. Blitum MADRASPATAN. Parietariæ folio, ſpicatum *Hort. noſt. Sicc.* B. 28. *Ray* H. Pl. Vol. 3. app. p. 242.

12. Coralloides epiſpongioſa PHILIPPENS. virgulis paucioribus punctatis, Sanguinei coloris. *Philipp.* Submar. Cat. 16. S. Act. Phil. N 286. p. 1421. 16. *Specimens of this and Figure* 8, *with ſeveral other very Curious Submarines, mentioned in that Tranſaction and Figured hereafter, were ſent me from the* Philippine Iſles *by the Learned Father* Kamel.

To FRANCIS ASTON, Eſquire, F. R. S. This *Table* is humbly dedicated by JAMES PETIVÈR, F. R. S.

GAZOPHYLACII NATURÆ & ARTIS, TAB. XXXII.

FIG. 1. Rete PHILIPPENSE nigrum, telis quadrangulis duplicatis *Phil.* Submar. Cat. 2. s. A. P. No 286. 1419.

2. Cochlea LUZONICA pallida, faſcià nigricante
2. Al-

3. Alcyonium PHILIPP. ramulis gelatinis implexis *Phil.* Submar. *Cat.* 8. s. *Act. Phil.* N 286. p. 1420. 8. *This is a very odd Submarine as is* Fig. 1. *both which I have given Descriptions of in the Transaction aforementioned.*

A. 4. Phalæna cinerea splendens maculata. *This differs from Fig.* 8. *below, in being larger and shining, and is not so commonly met with.*

5. Papilionoides CAROLINIANA fusca, signaturâ aureâ pellucidâ, subtus albidâ. *This is a new Genus of Exotick Insects (of which I have several sorts) its peculiarities are a thick and short Moth-like Body, its Horns turgid near the end but hook-pointed, and most of them have generally greater or lesser transparent coloured spots, it participates of the* Butterfly *and* Moth.

6. Papilio LIVONICUS è *fusco cærulescente, subtus maculatus.* Dr Nicolas Martini *a Curious young Gentleman, and son of the chief Physician of* Riga *gave me this when in* England, *with some other Insects which he had observed in* Livonia.

7. Phalæna-bombylus CAROLINIANUS maximus ferrugineus. *This is another new Genus of Insects, approaching next to the Hawk-moths, these suck their nutriment on the Wing like the humming Birds, are generally feather tail'd, and have a colourless transparency in the midst of their Wing:.*

A. 8. Phalæna minor alba, maculis nigrescentibus ornata. *an* Goed. Vol. 3, Tab. 13. p. Lift. Fig. 61. *This appears about* Midsummer *generally amongst* Nettles.

9. Concha LUZON. tubularis virescens. *The Natives in* Luzone *call this* Balay & Udpan, *and the* Spaniards *there* Boca de pato, *i. e.* Ducks-bill *from its shape. This I figured from a Shell Father* Kamel *sent me, since which in a* MSS *I have very lately received from him* DeConchyliis *I find both its Description and Delineations in other postures, with the addition of its Tube which shall be given you in my 2d Volume of* Decades.

10. Agrimonia MADRASPAT. folio rotundo singulari, subtus incano *Hort.* noft. *sicc:* A. 44. *Ray Hift.* Pl. Vol. 3. app. 241. *At the setting on of the* Leaves *its commonly attended with small tender auricles.*

11. Potamogiton MADRASPAT. Phyllitidis folio, pulchrè venoso *Hort.* noft. *sicc.* P. 65. *Ray* Vol. 3. app. 247. *The Veins on one side something resemble those of* Tab. 31: Fig. 6.   D 2

12. Leonurus MADRASPAT. foliis rigidis, parvis, hirtis *Hort.* noft. *Sicc.* L. 10. *Ray* Vol. 3. app. 246. *This differs from* Act. Phil. Nᵒ 244. p. 323. 21. *in being a smaller Plant, hoary, the* Leaves *lesser, shorter and stiff.*

To Mr JAMES AYREY, Merchant. This *Table* is humbly Dedicated by JAMES PETIVER, F. R. S.

GAZOPHYLACII NATURÆ & ARTIS, TAB. XXXIII.

FIG. 1. Lens MADRASPAT. Nummulariæ folio maculato *Hort.* noft. *Sicc.* L. 9. *Ray* V. 3. app. 246. *This is very remarkable both in its Leaves and Spots.*

2. Papilio LUSITAN. minor, ex aureo fuscus, subtus maculatus & virescens. Mr Jezreel Jones *caught this about* Lisbon *the laft day of* March 1698.

3. Scarabæus MARIANUS minor fulvus, maculis nigricantibus afperfis *Hift. Maryland.* s. *Act. Phil.* No 246. p. 396. 9. This refembles our common *English Lady-cow,* but hath much larger *Spots,* as that at *Table* 26. Fig. xi. has much lesser, and by mistake was there put down for this. Whereas that should have been called *Scarabæus stramineus minor* Marianus, *maculis aterrimis diversimode notatus* Act. Phil. No 246. p. 396. xi.

4. Thea CHINENSIS Pimentæ *Jamaicenfis* fol. fl. Rofaceo fimplici. *Chufan.* Plant. *Hift.* pl. 93. s. *Act. Phil.* No 246. p. 396. 93. *Where you may fee its* Description *and fome other* Remarks.

5. Papilio *Bella donna* dicta, VIRGINIANA. oculis fubtus majoribus. *This chiefly differs from our* English Painted Lady *Mufei noft.* 326. *in having larger Eyes underneath.*

A. 6. Phalæna Umbrica lineâ maculifq; fanguineis *an* Lift. Fig. 54. *an* prat. 3. *Moff.* 98. Fig. 97. id. A. 966. *This Moth produces a Catterpillar very common on* Ragwort, *and tho frequent, an elegant Infect.*

7. Phalæna GUINEENSIS alis è nigro aureis, corpore elegantiffimè zonato. *Its body is Girdled with Gold, Silver, Scarlet, Black and changeable, fo Beautiful I never yet in that part faw its like.*

8. An

8. Androsace CHUSAN. Cortusæ *Matthioli* folio *Muf.* noft. 858. *I take this elegant Plant to come next of kind to* Linum Umbilicatum, *which the accurate Botanift*, Dr Tournefort *calls* Omphalodes.

9. Cantharus CAROLIN. niger, undis pallefcentibus *Infect. Virgin. Obf.* No 36. s. *Act. Phil.* No 271. p. 813. 36. *This is of the Family of our* Green, Golden-fpotted *English* Cantharis.

A. 10. Phalæna nigrefcens maculis minoribus, fubtus fanguinea. *The Scarlet Royal Leopard.* I am oblig'd to Mr Antrobus *for this beautiful Infect, and remember to have fee it with Mr* Vernon.

11. Papilio CAROLIN. fufcus, fubtus cinereus, margine eleganter oculato. *I am much obliged to Madam* Williams *for this Curious Infect, which fhe fent me amongft many others caught, near her own Habitation in* Carolina.

A. 12. Phalæna nigrefcens, maculis majoribus, fubtus flavefcens. *Hollar* Tab. 4. fig. 7. *Jonf.* Infect. Tab. 8. Fig. 26. The Yellow Royal Leopard. *I have met with this about* London, *but rarely.*

To ROBERT BALLE, Efquire. This *Table* is humbly dedicated by JAMES PETIVER, F. R. S.

GAZOPHYLACII NATURÆ &ARTIS,TAB.XXXIV.

FIG. 1. Ageratum CAPENSE Crithmi folio, capitulis parvis. *Sent me from* Dr Fred. Ruyfch.

2. Hermannia CAPENSIS Altheæ folio *Hort.* noft.*Sicc.* H. 15. *Ray* H. Pl. V. 3. app. 245. *A fair Specimen of this* Mr John Starremburg *fent me amongft many others from the* Cape of Good Hope.

3. Ricinus CHINENSIS Sebifera, Populi nigræ fol. *Muf. noft.* 965. China Tallow-tree *le Compte* Angl. p. 101. *Who defcribes this Tree pretty well, and fays its red Leaves and white Kernels at a diftance, make a very fine profpect: See it's other* Synonyms *and* Defcription *amongft the* Chufan Plants, *I have given an Account of in the* Philofoph. Tranfactions No 286. p. 1427. 90.

4. Nerita ORCADENSIS lutea, bifafciis nigris.

5. Nerita ORCAD. fufca, fafciâ unicâ flavefcente.

6. Nerita ORCAD. flava, ftriis capillaceis. *Thefe* 3 *elegant varieties, my kind Friend* Mr Will. Clerk Surgeon, *found the laft Summer on the Shoars of the* Orkney Ifles.

A. 7. Papilio minor, è fufco & aureo quodammodo teffellatus. *The Checkered Hogg.* This and the next are fuppofed *Male* and *Female.*

A. 8. Papilio minor, ex aureo & fufco mixtus, ftriâ nigrâ notabili. *The Checker-like Hogg.* This is known from the laft in having 2 black ftreaks, near the Shoulders of its upper Wings, and its Golden Checkers in this are here lefs obvious, and rather melted into a Field.

A. 9. Papilio minor, aureus, ftriâ nigrâ diftinctus. *The ftreakt Golden Hogg.*

A. 9. a. Papilio minor aureus immaculatus. *The Spotlefs Hogg.* Here needs no Figure of this, it only wanting the ftreak in the laft. *Thefe four varieties the Curious* Mr Dandridge *has both obferv'd and plainly diftinguifht.*

10. Faba ORCAD. nigra, polita, tetrafculcata, hilo magno. *vid.* Cluf. *Exot.* p. 4. Fig. 9. *My Ingenious Friend* Mr James Wallace, Phyfician, *hath* Figured *this in his Defcription of the* Orckney Ifles, p. 14. *from whofe Shoars* Mr Will. Clerk *brought it me.* Father Kamel *hath alfo fent me the fame from the* Philippine Ifl:s.

11. Agnus Caftus CROCOD. folio glauco fubrotundo. *When I firft received this, which was from the* Crocodile Ifles. *I took it for a fort of* Teucrium, *fomewhat like the* Bæticum Clufii, *its Leaves and Flowers refembling it : but fince I have obtained better Specimens from* Chufan, *by the Fruit I find it to be a true* Agnus Caftus ; *I alfo take it to be the fame that* Mr Ray *defcribes from* Father Kamel *in the Appendix to his* 3d *Volume.* p. 72. 3. *who fays its rarely trifoliated, as the famples I have yet feen are fo.*

12. Arenaria minor Camphoratæ folio. *Lychnis pumila faxatilis* Juniperi folio *Elem. Botan.* 281. Inft. *Rei* Herb. 339. 2. *This Specimen with feveral others, were fent me from* Monf. Vaillant, *Secretary to* Dr Fagon, *chief Phyfician to the* King of France.

To Dr JOHN COATSWORTH, Phyfician at Sr Albans. This *Table* is humbly dedicated by JAMES PETIVER, F. R. S.

GAZOPHYLACII NATURÆ & ARTIS, TAB. XXXV.

A. FIG. 1. Papiliunculus cœruleus vulgatissimus *Muf. noft.* 318. The blue Argus. *Very common in* Heaths.

A. 2. Papiliunculus cœrulescens, limbis nigris. *The pale blue Argus.* This is somewhat larger, than the last, and much paler on both sides. *I have observed it in the* Thickets *near* Banstead Downs, *and in the like places about* Purfleet *near* Gravesend.

A. 3. Papiliunculus è cœruleo fuscus. *The mixt Argus.* This differs from Fig. 1. in having brown mixt with the blue, and some Eyes on the margent of the lower Wings above.

A. 4. Papiliunculus fuscus, marginibus aureis. *The edg'd brown Argus.* This has no blue above, but selvidg'd with Golden Eye-like Spots.

5. Curculio BENGALENSIS subrufus maximus. *This is much the largest Insect of this kind, I ever saw, I cannot perceive any Mouth it has, but that deficiency, Nature I presume, has made up with its Snout or Proboscis, which being hollow, sucks in its nourishment.* Mr John Fox, Surgeon, *brought me this with other Insects from the* Bay of Bengall.

A. 6. Buccinulum minimum ovale. *an* Buccinum exiguum subflavum, mucrone obtuso *sive* Cylindraceum *Lift. Hift. Anim. Angl.* 121. Fig. 6. *I have found this very small Shell on the sandy Banks of the* River Thames *near* Kingston, *it's distinguisht from others, by being thick, short and blunt.*

7. *Vaccinia* forte CHUSAN. Laurocerasi fol. fl. tubuloso. *I am obliged to that worthy Communicative Gentleman* Dr Sloane, *for Specimens of this Tree with its Flowers.*

A. 8. Planorbis minimus, Algis frequenter adnascens. *an* Vermiculus exiguus albus, Nautiloides *Algæ* ferè adhærens *Lift.* H *Conch.* L. 4. S. 3. Fig. 5. Tab. 533. *It's found on our own and Neighbouring Sea Shoars.*

A. 9. Schistus Pinoides major. *This and the next to fill up the cavity of their impressions have a* Coal-like *substance in many of them, they somewhat resemble the* Scales *of* Pine-cones *or their younger Branches.*

A, 10.

A. 10. Schiftus Pinoides minor. *The impreffions on this are much fmaller than the laft, they were both found in a* Coale Pit *at* Northbyerly *in* Yorkfhire, *and famples fent me from thence, from my Curious Friend,* Dr Rich. Richardfon *a Learned Phyfitian in that Town.*

11. Rofa CHUSAN. glabra, Juniperi fru¢tu. *This Rofe I have received both from* Chufan *and* China, *but not with Fruit, till* Dr Sloan *was pleaf'd to give it me.*

12. Myriophyllon INDIÆ ORIENT. ramofiffimum, *Philipp.* fubmar. *Cat.* 6.'s. A. P. No 286. *an* Abies maritima coralloides pennata, fubhirfuta *Breyn.* Prodr. 2. p. 1. 1. Fig. 3 ?

13. *A fragment of the laft, as it appears thro the* Microfcope *and mentioned in the* A. P. No 286. p. 1420. 6.

To SIR GODFRY COPLEY, Baronet and F. R. S. This *Table* is humbly dedicated by JAMES PETIVER, F. R. S.

GAZOPHYLACII NATURÆ & ARTIS, TAB. XXXVI.

FIG. 1. Gramen Lagopoides CHUSAN. fpicis criftatis pallefcentibus *Chufan.* 24. s. A. P. No 286. p. 1322. 24.

2. Sambuco paluftri affinis JAPONENS. fol. lato, ferrato, flore cæ:ulefcente *Hort.* noft. *Sicc.* S. 8. Ray H. Pl. V. 3. app. 248.

A. 3. Papilio minor, fufcus HAMSTED. marmoreatus. *Handleys brown Butterfly.* This varies fomething in magnitude and colour, out fcarce difcernable.

4. Os pulchre ferratum, forfan *Pifcis* cujufdam. *I am obliged to* Mr James Robertfon, Apothecary, *for this odd Bone, fince which* Mr Will. Hayes brought *me another fome what larger and lefs ferrated, from the* Eaft Indies.

A. 5. Mufca Apiformis probofcide porre¢to, alis ma-culatis. *This hovers in the Air like a* Hawk *and darts with a wonderful fwifnefs.*

A. 6. Pap. fufcus, &c. *Muf.* noft. 325. *Our brown Marfh Fritillary.* This and Fig. 9. I take to be *Male* and *Female.* They are not common.

7. Coccifera CHUSAN. Coryli folio, floribus exiguis racemiferis *Chuj.* 67. A. P. No 286. p. 1423. 67. *The Figures of this Plant and the next, were taken from* Dr Sloan's Specimens. 8. Fa-

8. Fagara CHUSAN. Rhois Virginianæ fol. caule a-lato *Chuf.* 74. A. P. No 286. p. 1423. 74. *This is known from the reft of this Tribe by its welted ftalks, fee my Remarks on 2 or 3 forts in the aforefaid* Tranfaction, *fince which I have received feveral other kinds of it from thofe parts.*

A. 9. Papiliunculus fufcus. punctis paucioribus albicantibus. *Mr Dandridges* Marfh Fritillary. *The Spots on this are larger and fewer than Fig.* 6.

A. 10, Phalæna-bombylus maximus ruffus. *That accurate Obferver* Mr Jofeph Dandridge *was the firft difcoverer of this large and beautiful Infect, who caught it about the end of* May *at the foot of* Box-hill.

A. 10. a Phalæna-bombylus max. fufcus. *This and the laft may be* Male *and* Female, *its dark part of the Wings are blacker and narrower,* Mr Rand *caught this the laft Summer on* Hampftead Heath.

11. Cochlea ORCAD. maxima, craffa, fafciata. *This refembles our* Scarborow Covins *Muf. noft.* 813. but 4 times bigger.

12. Echinus CHINENS. ftellatus, compreffus. *Mr* James Cuningham *found this elegant* Sea Urchin *on the* Coaft of China.

To Dr PHILIP HORNECK, Phyfician at EXON. This Table is humbly dedicated by JAMES PETIVER, F. R. S.

GAZOPHYLACII NATUR. & ARTIS, TAB. XXXVII.

FIG. 1. Phalæna LUZON. media è nigro alboque mixta. *This is black and white as the* Figure *reprefents.*

2. Chryfalis parva, caftanea, Erucæ fequentis. *From this breaks out the* Moth Figured *in* Tab. 28. 8.

3. Eruca LUZON. pilofa antennulata, nigro & flavo variata, Soncho lævi victitans. *This Catterpillar having fpun a filken Webb coffin'd (i. e. changed into its* Chryfalis) *the* 16th *of* October, *and flew the* 22d *of the fame month.*

4. Orobanche MAURITANICA, fl. purpureo. *Grows in* Sandy *places, to the* Broom *at* Fig. 13, *it* Flowers *in* Feb. *and* March, *the Inhabitants call it* Danoon. *This* Plant *with many others were obferved and defigned by* Mr John James *a Surgeon, about the year* 1680. Whilft he

was

was in *Barbary*, being a Slave there near 20 years, and after his Death this Book fell into the Hands of my very kind Friend, *Mr John Thorpe, Apothecary* in *Wapping*, who was generously pleas'd to make me a Present of it.

5. Papilio LUZON. medius albus. *This and the first are from Designs Father* Kamel *sent me.*

6. Scarabæus Cerambix LUZON. facie Tauri. *Of this, the next, and* Fig. 12. F. *Kamel* sent me both the *Designs* and *Insects.*

7. Stockerus LUZON. viridis, scapulâ maculisq; purpureis. *This is an elegant Species of* Tab. 21. Fig. 12. *Where I have described its peculiarity.*

8. Fructus pent-angulus, alte sulcatus unucleus. Mr Edward Bulkley *first procured me this* Fruit, and *from* Cochin-china *Mr Cuninghame* hath lately sent it me.

9. Curçuma *Officinarum* Dale Pharm. 362. 5. *Kamel* Ray H. Pl. Vol. 3. app. 23 xi. The true *Turmerick.* For its *Synonyms* I refer you to Mr *Dale*, and its Native Names and particular Virtues, to *F. Kamel*, who adds, that tho *Matthiolus, Cordus* and others, have made them to differ in their *Roots*, viz. *Round* and *Long*, yet they are both the same, the 1st, the Mother or Tuberous Glands, the *Long* only its offspring.

10. Nucleus tetragonus GUINEENSIS, basi foraminoso. *Its of a Woody substance with capillary Veins, has at the bottom 2 large holes near the length of the Fruit.*

11. Nux LUZONICA fusca, zonâ pallidâ. *I received this amongst some other* Fruit, Shells, &c. *from* F. Kamel *and by his description it seems to be the Kernel of* the Arbor Bigaâ, Ray H. Pl. V. 3. app. 61. 3.

12. Cerambix LUZON minor atratus & striatus.

13. Spartium MAURITANICUM, fl. albo monospermos. *This in* Arabic *they call* Rotum, *I take it to be the same that I have once received from* Cales, *viz.* the Spartum 3. Hispa 1. *Clusij* Hisp. 207. Fig. & *Hist.* 103. Fig. *which the* Spaniards *call* Retama.

To Dr JOHN HUTTON, Physician. This *Table* is humbly dedicated by JAMES PETIVER, F. R. S.

GAZOPHYLACII NATUR. & ARTIS, TAB. XXXVIII.

FIG. 1. Nux GUINEENSIS, nucleo Mofchatæ fimilis. *The* Shell *of this is thick and brittle, in fhape like the* Kernel *of the* Nutmeg, *which is the part we ufe, the* Kernel *of this within, is the colour of* Palm Oyl, *and the confiftence of* Suet.

2. Phafeolus JAMAICENSIS, niger, compreffus, circa hilum albus. *an* Phafeolus maximus perennis, femine compreffo lato, nigris maculis notato, *Cat. Pl. Jam. 66. There are* Beans *in* I. B. V. 1. L. 17. p. 267. *and* 8. *refembling this but not exactly.*

3. Nucleus LUZON. Dactyli facie, fere trifpermos.

4. Nucleus LUZON. Cylindraceus, fulcatus, extremitatibus punctatis. *This and the laft are* 2 *very odd* Fruits, *both which I received from* Fath. Kamel.

5. Scarabæus arboreus LUZON, 3. feu fubplanus fubluftris luridé æruginofe maculofus *Kamel Mfs. This is next of kind to our* Table 23. Fig. 12. *and* Tab. 26. 9. *This In fect and the following I have received from him, fince the Manufcript he fent me, which I intend e're long to publifh.*

5. Scarabæus arboreus LUZON. 2. f. luteo-fufcus, tenuiter ftriatus *Kam. Mfs.* Our Bracken-clock *Figured* Tab. 22. 4. *is like this, but lefs.*

7. Ægilops MAURITANICA, ariftis longioribus binis *Hort. Sicc. Petiver.* A. 37. *Ray* H. Pl. V. 3. app. 241. *This the* Moors *call* Khortaan, *and flourifhes in* May. *Its* Defcription, *with the 2 next and* Fig. 12. *I hope fuddenly, to give you, with fome others from the fame place.*

8. Sanamunda *forte* MAURITANICA, fl. luteo. *It* Flowers *all* Winter *and Seeds in* March, *the* Natives *call it* Mittinaam, *which Mr* Jezreel Jones *tells me fignifies ftrong, perhaps from its* Bark, *of which they make* Cords *and* Ropes, *as we do of* Hemp.

9. Chamæciftus *forte* MAURITANICA, luteus, foliis parvis ferratis. *From a Fibrous* Root *it fendeth up a ftem* 3 *inches high.*

10. Papiliunculus LUZON. cœrulefcens, fubtus undis ftriatus.

11. Scarabæus arboreus LUZON. fubluftris punctatus *Salibamban* & *Salagabat* Indis. *This* Father Kamel *fent me*
                                                              amongft

amongst his other Designs, but I have not yet received the Insect from him.

12. Carlina forte MAURITAN. fl. ex albo sanguineo. *The* Natives *call it* Tickuntoos. *It* Flowers *in* April. *The* Roots *are of a very hot taste, and by them much used in* Powder *and* Conserve, *to heat the coldness of the Stomach.*

To Mr FRANCIS MOULT, Chymist. This *Table* is humbly dedicated by JAMES PETIVER, F. R. S.

GAZOPHYLACII NATUR. & ARTIS. TAB. XXXIX.

FIG. 1. Baccifera planta perpumila MAURITANICA. *This grows in Rocky Mountainous places, and is by the* Moors *called* Fox-grapes.

2. Dracunculus volans Looganus, ex sicco desumptus. *This seems to differ from that I have mentioned in my* Museum No 119. *in being speckled, and having 6 ribs in each* Wing, *ours having but* 4, *and instead of little spots is largely waved with dark brown.*

3. Ficoides forte MAURITAN. perexigua. *The* Natives *call this* Lowon.

4. Papilio LUZON. fuliginosus, oculatus & undulatus. *Besides its dull colour this is distinguisht by having 6 Eyes in each lower Wing.*

5. Papilio LUZON. fuscus minor, ter varie bioculatus. *The Eyes in the Wings of this Fly are peculiarly placed.*

6. Eruca LUZON. multicolor. *Eruca* Malvæ hortens. polymita, glabra, albo, fusco, nigro & flavo tessellatim variegata *Kamel Mss. This changed into a* Chesnut Chrysalis *Fig.* 7. *the* 19th *of* Feb. *which produced the* 3d *of* March, a variegated Moth like *Dr Listers* No 92.

7. Chrysalis ultimæ Erucæ.

8. Fungus MAURITANICUS verrucosus ruber, succo sanguineo. *Turtooths Bargasham* Indigenis. *It grows a foot high, of a dark red but paler below.*

9. Locusta echinata impennis è CHUSAN. *I am obliged to Mr* Ja. Cuninghame *for this odd Insect, which somewhat resembles the* Locusta-talpa *Tab.* 13. Fig. 7.

10. Rot-

10. Rottang LUZON. vulgaris. *Fructus* peregrinus fquamofus 3. *Cluf. Exot.* 24. Fig. 2. *I take this to be the* Fruit *of the* common Rottang, *which I have given the* Synonyms *of, &c. in my* Unaneercoonda *Collection of* Plants *in* Act. Phil. No 244 p. 326. pl. 27. F. Kamel *hath fent a Defcription of it,* vid. Ray H. Pl. V. 3. app. 19. 3.

10. a. Officulum *Ejufdem. This* Stone *is horny, the* Meat white and flimy, *of a grateful fowre, chewed quenches Thirft, a Tea or Decoction of it refrefhes Feverifh Perfons, and is effectual in heat of the Reins.*

11. Rottang LUZON. fructu pyramidali majore *Labnit* Kamel. *Ray* H. Pl. V. 3. p. 19. 4.

11. a. *Its* Kernel *which is alfo edible, is of a Tart Sweetnefs.*

12. Eruca LUZON. radiata, a; pilis plumofa. *Eruca* ardens *Bafut* Kam. Mfs. *The middle of the Back is yellow, fpotted with black, the Body green, from whence and its fides, comes 20 hairy Feathers, it feeds on the* Rofe. *This is a very odd* Caterpillar, *and its* Coffin *as ftrange being globular.*

13. Aurelia LUZON. globofa fufca. *It's about the bignefs of a* Pea, *and is the* Coffin *of the laft* Caterpillar, *into which it changed the* 17th *of* January *and the* 18th *of* Feb. *following produc'd a fmall brown* Moth, *like the* 2d *in* Aldrovand *de Infect.* his 10th Table.

To the Honourable ISAAC NEWTON, Efq; Prefident of the Royal Society. This *Table* is humbly dedicated by JAMES PETIVER, F. R. S.

GAZOPHYLACII NATURÆ & ARTIS, TAB. XL.

FIG. 1. Globularia MAURITAN. caule foliofo. *Tufolkha* Maurit. *It Flowers in* March.

2. Kali *forte* MAURITAN. polyfpermos.

3. Phalæna BENGALENSIS fufco & diaphano mixta. *This elegant Moth was caught* Decemb. 1701. *in the Bay of* Bengall, *by Mr* Henry Smith, *a Perfon I am obliged to for feveral new and Curious Infects he met with at Sea in that Bay and the Streights of* Malacca.

4. Papilio MADRASPATAN. croceus, nigris maculis afperfis, albifque ferie marginatus *Muf. noft.* 721. The *Madras* Fritillary.

5. Matricaria MAURITAN. pumila. *It Flowers in* April.

6. Culex LUZON. e viridi fufco. *Mufca* roftrata feu
Mufca-

Musca-Papilio Arbor *Lanette* Kam. Mss. Insect. *I take this to be of the Gnat kind by its make, and motion in Flying, which is very swiftly up and down.*

7. Cimex LUZON. oblongus è nigro & fusco,humeris echinatis. *Musca* Tympanista, s. Formica-Culex *Kam.* Mss. *This and the last frequent the* Lanette Tree, *described by Mr* Ray *in the Appendix to his* 3d *Volume, pag.* 89. 18. *I have observed one or two of this Genus of Insects in* England, *tho not Spinose.*

8. Aloes *forte* MAURITAN. pumila, foliis glaucis.

9. Yguana LUZON. edulis, capite cœrulescente. *Cagasagam* vel *Layagan* Indigenis. *It agrees with the* Yguana, *commonly called* Guana *in the* West Indies, *in being firm'd on the back, and edible. The Crest on its head is fleshy and red like a Cocks-Comb. Father* Kamel *has sent me an accurate Description of this, with several other* Lizards, *and also* Serpents, Frogs, Turtles, &c. *which e're long shall be publish'd.*

10. Convolvulus *forte* MAURITAN. fl.cœruleo,fundo luteo. *It Flowers in* May.

11. Phalæna Accipitrina LUZON. pulchra, variis coloribus ornata. *This was hatcht in a fortnight from the Aurelia or Coffin at* Fig. 13.

12. Eruca Elephantina LUZON. virescens maculis 4. flavis oculatis. *This Catterpillar eats the great* Philippine Arum *called there* Biga, *It's described by* Mr Ray *in his H. Pl. Vol. 3. app. 35. 1. Whose Figure I shall give in my 2d Volume of* Decades. *I find this, tho a biting Plant, a peculiar Food to 2 or 3 of these horned Caterpillars; before this changed into* Fig. 13. *which was* Feb. 14. *it turned from Green to Reddish, and on the 28th broke out into the Moth above.*

13. *This is the* Aurelia, Chrysalis *or Coffin of the last Catterpillar, viz. a middle state between it, and the Moth* Fig. 11. *which is the Insect in perfection.*

14. Anacardij ORIENTALIS *Officinarum* Fructus. *This is the dry Fruit of the true* Anacardium, *hitherto very rarely to be met with in our* Druggists Shops. *I first received it from* Persia, *where they use it in dying their* Chints *or Calicoes, which* Christ. Acosta & Garcias ab Horto *confirms. I have obtained Specimens of its Leaves and Flowers, which shall be Figured in my future* Decades.

To Sigr. JOHN FRANCIS VIGANI, Professor in Chymistry. This *Table* is humbly dedicated by JAMES PETIVER, F. R. S.

The following Perfons, have been my late Benefactors.

1. TO Mr Edward Bulkley *at* Fort St George, *I am again obliged for* 20 *Books of dry Plants, with some Seeds and Insects, amongst the first are some New, which I shall suddenly publish.*

2. Since my *Account* of the *Chusan Plants* Printed in the *Phil. Transact.* No 286. sent from *Mr James Cuninghame*; this curious Perfon hath again been pleased to favour *Dr Sloan* and me, with above 100 others from thence,(most of them since mentioned in my *Hortus Siccus Ray* H. Pl. Vol. 3 app. p. 241.) and very lately with about as many from the Kingdom of *Cochinchina,* as also several from *Pulo Condore,* to which he has added divers *Insects, Shells* and other *Curiosities,* of which e're long there shall be an account given.

3. *Dr John Crasto Hiegel,* Chief Physician to the *Archbishop* and *Elector of Tryers,* hath lately sent me some rare *Fossils* found in those parts, and amongst them the famed *Hysterolithos,* which I have figured in my 6th *Decade.*

4. I am obliged to *Mr Isaac Teal,* Apothecary General, for his care of these from so curious a Correspondent.

5. The Reverend and Learned *Father Kamel* alias *Camel,*besides his two Curious Treatises of the *Philippine Herbs* and *Trees,* formerly sent (which are now Printed in the 3d Volume of that late accurate Botanist, *Mr John Ray,* his Excellent *History of Plants)* hath again very lately been pleased to favour me with many Additions, new Observations and Delineations, both to his *Herbs* and *Trees,* as also a 3d Book *de Plantis Philippensibus,* part of which I have already inserted in the *Phil. Transact.* No 293. Where you will find such of them and the Herbs of which he sent me the Designs, (the Trees you shall see elsewhere) Several of these I have already *Figured* in my *Gazophylacick Tables,* and shall continue them, if this *Curious Age* will give encouragement; which is humbly hoped, since there are in them many *Discoveries* in all parts of *Nature,* which hitherto was never known to *Europe,* The same hath also sent me a *Treatise* of *Shells,* new discoveries in *Insects,* with many other *Curiosities.*

6. Dr John Jacob Scheuchzer, *Physician* at *Zurich,*and Fellow of the *Royal Society* in *England.* This accurate *Observer* of *Nature,* hath been pleased to present me with a Collection of rare *Alpine Plants* very neatly preserv'd, and in a very curious Mss. which he hath Dedicated and sent to the *Royall Society,* there are many of the Plants very finely Painted, which I will suddenly give the *Figures* of.

7. My Worthy Friend *Dr Sloan,* Physician, *Secretary* to the *Royall Society,* &c. hath been pleased to give me the freedom to *Figure* several of his infinite number of *Curiosities,* which will be no small Addition and Ornament to my future *Decades;* whose *Museum* since the late famous *Mr Courtine* alias *Charlton,* has added his entire Collection to it, may equal, if not exceed, most *Cabinets* in *Europe.*

8. *Dr Christian Maximilianus Spener,* Physician to the *King of Prussia,*and Fellow of the Royall *Brandenburgh* College of Sciences, as also one of the *Imperial Academy* of Curious Naturalists : To this *Worthy Person,* I am very sensibly obliged for a Box of curious *Fossils* sent the last *Summer,* and another lately received; a *Catalogue* of both, with *Figures* of the most rare shall suddenly be publish'd.

Several other *Benefactors* for want of room here, must be referred until the next opportunity.

ADVERTISEMENT.

THE *Tables* for the next *Decade* are all ready finish'd, and shall be publish'd as soon as 10 *Guineas* are Subscribed; in these, amongst other Curious things, you will see the *Figures* of the

1. Cortex Peru *or* Jesuits Bark, *with its* Leaves, *&c:*
2. *Several* Plants *from* Barbary.
3. *Divers* Philippine Insects.
4. Amomum legitimum *Kameli* Ray Vol. 3. Dend. 89
5. Pao de Cobra *or* Snakewood.
6. *Some* Indian Fruits.
7. A singular Water Fowl.
8. *A rare sort of the* Fish *Remora*.
9. *Divers* elegant Beetles, *some very large.*
10. A Circular impression on *Stone* from *Dr Spener.*
11. *Vanillia* with its *Leaves* and elegant *Flowers.*
12. *Shells* from several parts.
13. Some Beautiful *Birds.*
14. Several *Philippine Trees.*
15. *Exotick* submarine Bodies as *Coral*, &c.
16. A long tailed *Fruit*, found in the Ships taken at *Vigo*, which the *Spaniards* in *Mexico* use in their *Chocolate.*
17. Divers elegant *Ferns* from F. *Kamel.*
18. Some Shells from *Pulo Condore* from *Mr Cuninghame.*
19. A Scarlet *Philippine* Fungus.
20. *English Insects* hitherto undescribed.
21. *A strange* Centaur-like Monster, from the *Philippines.*
22. A singular *Visco Aloes* from those parts.
23. The *Wood* and *Leaf* of an *Indian* Counterpoison.
24. *Exotick Insects*, many very Beautiful.

With several other things, no less rare, which for want of room here, we must refer you to the Decade itself.

N. B. I am putting to the *Press* the 11th and 12th *Centuries* of my *Museum*, containing *English Insects and Shells*, and of the last many Foreign, with divers *Indian Plants*, never yet known to be described by any *Author.*

And in a little time, God permitting me Health, I design to give a *Catalogue* of many *British Fossils*, and with them several others which I have lately received from my *kind Friends* abroad; and if they, or other *Curious Persons*, will be so kind suddenly to furnish me with more, I will both mention and retalliate their Favours conferred on their Humble Servant, JAMES PETIVER.

Aldersgate street, March 15. 1704. LONDON.

Sold by Mr *Smith* and Mr *Bateman*, Booksellers.

GAZOPHYLACII
NATURÆ & ARTIS
DECAS QUINTA:

In quâ ANIMALIA, FOSSILIA, PLANTÆ,
Omniaque Rariora ARTE producta

DESCIPTIONIBUS brevibus,& ICONIBUS illustrantur.

A JACOBO PETIVER, Pharmacop. *LONDINENSI,*
& REGIÆ SOCIETATIS Socio.

GAZOPHYLACII NATURÆ
& ARTIS, TAB. XLI.

FIG. 1 *Cimecoides* LUZONIS Hortensis, ex viridi, flavo, albo, nigro & rubro, eleganter de-
picta. *This feeds on the* Lupine leaved Malabar
Rattle-Broom.

2. *Scarabæus* pectenarius LUZON. merè viridis. *The*
Inhabitants call this Ticpaclong, *its of a pale shining green,*
and is of our Dor *or* Tree Beetle kind, *having Horns, when*
expanded, resembling a Comb. The next with this, *Father*
Kamel sent me amongst other *Curious Insects.*

3. *Cochinella* LUZON. *major e cupreo viridique eleganter*
striata. This is a very elegant Beetle, each Rib alternately streak'd with a changeable green and copper lustre.

I   *The*

The Curious Mr Charles Du Bois gave me fome years fince a leffer of this, fince which my kind Friend Mr *Jezreel Jones* hath brought it me from *Lisbon*.

4. *Jacobæa* MAURITANICA *Coronopi* folio. It Flowers *in* March.

5. *Mufca tricornis* LUZONICA. The Head and Body of this is black, the laft mixt with white, it hath a dancing Flight like our Gnats.

6. *Cimex* LUZON *omnino viridis*. I take Fig 1. to be the *Hexapode* of this *Lupine-Rattle Bugg*.

7. *Nodiflora* MAURITANICA *foliis verticilli modo ferratis*. It's found in *Barbary* amongft Rocks and Stoney places and heads in *February*.

8. *Amomum* legitimum *Komeli*. You may fee a large and accurate *Defcription* of this in the *Dendrology* of Mr *Ray*'s 3d Volume of *Plants*, p. 89. Thefe Seeds fmelling pleafantly, the Indian Maidens wear Bracelets of them about their Neck and Arms, mixt with *Musk Seed, Job's Tears, Indian Cane, Abrus* or *Angola* Seed, &c.

9. *Polygala* MAURITAN. *lutea aromatica*. This rare Plant, with Fig. 4 and 12. were obferved in *Barbary*, and taken from the defigns of an Herbal I have mentioned in Tab. 37. Fig. 4. which our kind Brother Mr *John Thorpe, Apothecary*, gave me.

10. *Phalæna* BENGALENSIS, fulva, maculâ albefcente. Mr Henry Smith *caught this in the Bay of* Bengale, *Decemb.* 1701. He alfo obferved the fame at *Malacca* the *March* following.

11. *Phalæna* BENGAL. *viridefcens, linea pallefcente*. Sent me with the laft. To this Gentleman I am particularly obliged for thefe and feveral other very curious Infects, he being a perfon I never yet faw.

12. *Limonium* MAURITAN. *flore minimo, caule foliofo*. The *Barbary Sea Lavander*. It *Flowers* in *May*.

To the *Right Honourable* THOMAS Lord Vifcount WEYMOUTH. This *Table* is humbly *Dedicated* by JAMES PETIVER, F. R. S.

GAZOPHYLACII NATURÆ & ARTIS. TAB. XLII.

FIG. 1. Pao de Cobra *Lusitanis*, i. e. Snakewood. *Father Kamel* says this is brought from *India*, its *Bark* is reddish, thin, compact and bitterer than the Wood, which is grey and solid, resembling that of *Tamarisk*, vid. Ray Syllab. *Kamel*. p. 88. 6.

2. Scarabæus *pectinarius* LUZON. *capite dentato*. The Squill Comber. *Feeding on that Plant.*

3. Scarabæus LUZON. *forcipatus ater*. This gnaws Trees. The last and this I have Samples of.

4. *Nux bifotis in tres dehiscens putaminis partes*. Under this inscription *Father Kamel* sent me its design, with Fig. 8, 10 and 14. amongst several other *Fruits*, which you will see in my following *Decades*.

5. Pilularis LUZON. *niger minimus*. Fig. 2, 3, and this, were sent me amongst the Designs of *Fath. Kamel's Philippine Beetles*, and since that the Insects themselves of the 2 last.

A. 6. Phalæna Bombylus, *parvus, corpore nigro, ano cineceo*. This is curiously preserved in *Mr Joseph Dandridge's Collection*, who caught it in *Hornsey Wood* in *June*.

7. *Jasmini flore, frutex* PHILIPPENSIS, *Foliis Floribusque fere ternis*. Dicitur *dalaga Luzonensibus*. It grows on the Sea Coasts; the *Leaves* stink and taste like *Wormwood*. Kamel. Syllab. seu *Raii* Hist. Plant. Vol. 3. append. Pag. 92. No. 46.

8. Nux NAICENSIS 2. *Setis candidis convestita* Fig. 14. and this F. *Kamel* supposes to be *Nuts* of *Palms*. Kam. Syllab. Ray p. 46. No 19.

A. 9. *Musca* Apiformis, *proboscide porrecto, alis non maculatis*. This differs from *Gaz. Natur.* Tab. 36. Fig. 5. in being somewhat less, the *Wings without Specks*, but more clouded on its upper edge. Mr Dandridge *observed this in* Caın Wood.

10. *Nux Moschata* oblonga, maxima, montis *Balete*. Father Kamel *sent me this draught, and from him it's described by* Mr Ray *in his* Syllabus *pag.* 58. 4. *Its Leaves, Kernel and exterior Fruit, you shall have the* Figures of *amongst the* Philippine Trees *with the* Male and Female Nutmegs.

A. 10. A. Phalæna *parva viridescens, corpore fusco* I have as yet seen this Insect only in Mr Dandridge's Collection Its brown Body and pale Rim differs it from the next.

A. 11. Phalæna *parva, viridefcens, corpore albefcente.* Several of thefe I have obferved in a *Wood* againft the *Boarded River* after *Midfummer.*

A. 12. *Aurelia* nigrefcens *Ejufdem.*

A. 13. Eruca *exigua lutea, capite & guttulis nigris.* This is the *Caterpillar* of Fig. 11. the Defigns and Obfervations of whofe changes we owe to the aforefaid Mr *Dandridge.*

14. Nux NAI.ENSIS I. *Cortice nigro, reticula candida obdučta.* An *Baguidiet* Fructus Alexipharmacus? *Kamel* Syllab: *Ray* p. 46. 18. an *Fructus* reticulato corio coftans *Claf. Exotic.* cap. 11. p. 31. Fig.

To Sr RICHARD BULKLEY, Knight and Baronet. This *Table* is humbly *Dedicated* by JAMES PETIVER. F. R. S.

GAZOPHYLACII NATURÆ & ARTIS. TAB. XLIII.

FIG. 1. *Umbilicato folio Arbor* PHILIPPENS. Balanti *dicta.* They commend the *Root* of this in *Fluxes.* Kamel. Syllab. Ray 93. 5.

2. Platani *folio Arbor* Pofopofo PHILIPPENS. A midd'ing Tree, its Wood brittle and of little ufe. *Kam.* Syll. Ray. 89. 24.

3. Phalæna LUZON. *ex albo purpureo nigroque eleganter variegato.* Its Head and Rump yellow, Back black, and Shou'der Ring white.

4. Eruca LUZON. *glabra, lineis luteis, fufcis & albis.* Thefe yearly feed in great numbers on the *Pancratium meus* after the Rains.

5. Aurelia *ejufdem.* This *Coffin* of the *laft Caterpillar* changed about *Chriftmas,* and in 15 or 16 days broke out into the elegant *Moth* at Fig. 3.

6. Squilla *marina* LUZON. *major.* Indis *Manla* & *Tila.* Kamel *de Pifcibus Molufcis & Cruftaceis* Philippenfibus *in Actis Philofoph.* No 302 31 where defcribing its length he means for *bicubitalis,* biuncialis, which better agrees with the Figure that I copyed from his defign.

7. *Zapotl* nigrum. Jucatanenfibus *Ulz.* This is a very great fhady Tree. with thick dark fhining *Leaves.*

8. *Flos* aureus pentapetalus *Ejufdem.*

9. *Calyx* & perianthium *Floris præcedentis.*

10. Fructus

10. Fructus *ejusdem*. The *Pulp* of this *Apple* is *black* or *brown*, and tastes like a Plumb ; but before its ripe it pricks the mouth like *Arum*, It contains 5 or 6 horney Stones. *Vid*. Kamel. *Syllab*. Ray *Vol*. 3. p. 54. pl. 4.

11. *Angola* LUZON. Aceris *folio*. The brittle Tree. The Natives use the *Leaves* to procure easy delivery.

12. Ardea *exotica aurita*. This *Bird* is very remarkable for its 2 ear'd Tufts on the Head and wanting its back Toe. *Mr Ray's* Figure of the *Ardea cinerea minor* in his *Ornithology* Tab. 49. p. 279. somewhat resembles it. I copyed this from a Picture amongst Mr *Cleark's* Collection of Paintings.

13. Squilla *marina* LUZON. minima, seu *Formica mari*-na. Hipon vel Dilis *Kamel* de Piscibus Moluscis & Crustaceis *Philippens*. in Act Phil. No. 302. 5.

14. Araneus LUZON. *oblongus lutescens, longipes, ventre tenui geniculo in caudam distincto*, Kamel MSS. Asaneor.

15. Phalena LUZON. *aterrima, collo, cauda extremitatibusque alarum aureis*. These 3 last are from Designs *Father Kamel* sent me.

To CIRIL ARTHINGTON, Esq;. This *Table* is humbly *Dedicated* by his humble Servant JAMES PETIVER, *Apothecary* and F. R. S.

GAZOPHILACII NATURÆ & ARTIS. TAB. XLIV.

FIG. Abrus *minor coccineus vulg. hilo nigro*. I have received this Seed from *Africa* and both the *Indies*.

1. a. Abrus *lutescens*.

1. b. Abrus *niger*. These are varieties of the first.

2. Abrus ANTEGOANUS, *medius miniatus*.

3. Abrus ANTEG. *med. miniatus, nigro nubulatus*. Both these Mrs *Rachel Chapman* brought me from Antegoa.

4. Abrus *sanguineus maximus, nigro mixtus*, Anacock quibusdam.

5. Abrus BARBAB. *niger parvus, hilo rubro*. This *Pod* hath rarely more than 2 *Seeds*, and sometimes but one.

6. Semen *Ejusdem*. This is smaller than *Fig*. 1. flattish, black with a red Eye.

7. Cochlea *oblonga exotica levis*. I met with this at *Mad. York's*, and have not elsewhere seen it.

8. Pha

8. Phalæna *alba femidiaphana, guttulis paucis nigris.* I am obliged to Mr *Antrobus* for this rare *Gawfe Moth.*

9. Rhinoceros LUZON. *nigricans capite vaginifque punctulatus.* Father Kamel *was pleafed to prefent me with this Curious Beetle and its Defign.*

10. Bontiana LUZON. *geniculis inferioribus carinulatis.* Bontius *being the firft that gave us this kind, if not this Plant, I have attributed his Name to it for diftinction fake. Its a Parafitical Plant,* generally growing on *Trees as out* Polypodium and Mifleto, the Flowers *for the moft part refembling* Aloes or Orchis, *and by fome are therefore called* Vifco Aloes.

11. Sorbus LUZON. *foliis ternis ferratis.* Bitongol *Indis,* Carandas *Garciæ ex* Sententia *Kameli.* It *Flowers* in *May,* and *Fruit* ripens in *Auguft,* of a pleafant roughifh Sweetnefs, and full of fmall G ains.

12. Remora LUZON. *corpore tereti.* Comi *Boholanis* & *Zebuanis.* Quini *Leitenfibus.* This feems to differ from the common kind. *See its Defcription* with feveral other *Fifh* which *Father Kamel* has obferved about the *Philippine Ifles,* publifhed in a MSS he fent me in the *Philofophical Tranfactions,* No.302. 24.

13. Toucan SURINAMENSIS *niger, ex albo flavo rubrique mixta.* Taken from a *Dutch Painting* in Mr *Clark's Collection.* This does not exactly agree with any Authors I have yet read.

To Dr JOHN PHILIP BREYNIUS at *Dantzick* M. D. & S. R. S. This *Table* is humbly *Dedicated* by JAM. PETIVER, *Apothecary,* and F. R. S.

GAZOPHILACII NATURÆ & ARTIS. TAB. XLV.

FIG. 1. *Lignum* Arboris *Panguaguafon.* The *Root* and *Wood* of this is both a *Vulnerary* and *Febrifuge,* takes away Pains in the Head, is good againft Poifon and the Bites of Venamous Creatures, as has been experienced. Kam. Syllab. Ray p. 89. 16.

2. Folium *ejufdem.*

3. Concha Tiquafay *facies extera* Kam. MSS de *Teftac.* This is a fort of *Tree* or *Rock Oyfter,* and agrees with a *Virginia kind,* which from its fhape they call a *Hammer Shell.*

4. *Monstrum* PHILIP. *Centauri* facie. *F. Kamel* sent me a Design of this in a MSS *Tract de Monstris*, quasi *Monstris & Monstruosis*, which shall e're long be printed.

5. Phalæna *media rufescens*, Semicolon *dicta*. What is very particular in this Moth is, its under Wings, from its Shoulders are extended beyond the upper, which, with its Semicolon-like Speck, remarkably distinguishes it from all others.

6. Phalæna LUZON. *alba, margine superiore & corpore sanguineis.* F. *Kamel sent me a* Painting of this, and Mr *Cuninghame* a Moth very like it.

7. Nux Arboris *Hobom* quam & *Tagoligas* vocant. *Kamel* MSS.

8. Nucleus *Hobom.*

9. Zapotl CHINENS. *fructu cinnabarino.* Xicu *Sinens.* Chicoy *Hispan.* Figocaque *Lusit.* Its *Leaves* single, 6 inches long and 3 broad. *Kam.* Syll, *Ray* p. 54. 5.

10. Zapotl *Fructus.* These are dryed in the Sun, as they do *Figs* and so sent abroad.

11. Zapotl *Osficulum.*

12. Lapis *cui a Natura Curiosa figura insculpta est* D. Spener, *Act. Phil.* No 302. p. 2083. 16. This Dr *Christian Maximilian Spener, Physician to the King of Prussia, and Fellow* both of the *Imperial* and *Brandenburgh Colleges,* sent me. It seems to be an Impression of an *Entrochus* upon a sort of *Iron Stone.*

A. 13. Phalæna *brunna bimaculata fasciis fulvis.* This and Fig. 5. two very elegant Moths, my Curious Friend Mr *Antrobus* was pleased to give me amongst several other.

14. Buccinulum MEDITERRAN. *leve. ex albo nigroque variegatum.* I have received this from several Shoars in the *Streights,* and lately from our Worthy Friend Mr *Robert Ball,* sent him amongst other Shells from *Leghorn.*

To his *Curious Friend* Mr JOSEPH DANDRIDGE. This *Table* is humbly *Dedicated* by JAMES PETIVER, *Apothecary,* and F. R. S.

GAZOPHILACII NATURÆ & ARTIS TAB. XLVI.

FIG. 1. Serpens AMERICAN. *variegatus, cingulis maculisque nigris interserfis.*

2. Vanillia *Officinarum.* Dale *Pharm.* 508. This *Figure* shews its *Leaves* and twin or double *Pods,* with its manner of twining about other Plants.

3. *Vanillia,* its *Flower,* which being so particular may easily be known from other Plants.

4. Its full grown *Pod,* which is used in *Chocolate,* and and has the fragrancy of *Benjamin.*

5. Betle MEXICAN. *repens fol. pinguibus odoratis.* This the *Natives* call *Mecaxochitl,* they mix it with their *Chocolate* to give it a more pleasant Taste and correct the Breath.

6. Betle NOVÆ HISPAN. *fructu longo angustissimo.* There was several of these found in the Spanish West India Ships, when destroyed at *Vigo.* Dr Sherard *new Consul of Smyrna* gave me some of them: They have generally 2 and sometimes 3 Tails tyed together, with a Twine, which seems to be the Splinter of some sort of *Rush.*

7. Unicornu NEVICENSE, *gyris cavis.* This Shell is very particular in having alternate hollows round its Twirls, which in the *Figure* is exprest by the black Spots.

8. Arbor MEXICANA, *flore* Tulipæ, *staminibus* Ornithopodij *simile.* Macpalxochi quahuitl *Mexicanis.* Flor Camochano *Hispanis.* This is a very odd Tree; I shall think my self very much obliged to any one that shall be pleased to send me Samples of it, or any Plant like it.

9. Arbor PERUVIANA, *Corticem* Febrifugam *ferens.* I took this from a *Figure* in *Monsieur Pomet* his *Hist.* of *Drugs* in *French:* I will give a Guinea to the first Person that brings or sends me fair Specimens of its *Leaves, Flower* and *Fruit,* or any 2 of them on the same Branch.

10. and 11. Are the external and internal face of the Bark of the aforesaid Tree.

12. Avicula *forte* SURINAMENS. *e nigro rubroque mixta.* It's behind mostly black, the *Head, Collar, Breast* and *Belly* red.

13. Avi-

13. Avicula *forte* SURINAM. *nigra, capite e luteo croceo.* I take this and the last to be *Surinam Birds.* I copyed them from *Paintings* which *Mr Clark* brought from *Holland.*

14. Scarabæus MEXICAN. bicornis. Tomolin ich-catzin *Mexicanus.* The lighter part in this Figure is of a reddish Chefnut colour, the rest black.

15. Papiliunculus *exoticus cærulefcens.* This is a Stranger to me: I joyn it with these Birds, becaufe they feem to make it their prey.

16. Echinites CAROL. *compreffus rhomboidibus Teftudinaribus.* This is a piece of *Foffil Echinus*, and feems much to refemble that *Figured* No 125. in my *Mufeum*, which I lately defcribed in the Philofoph. Tranfact. No. 299.

To Dr JOHN CRAFTO HIEGEL, *Chief Phyfician* to the *Elector* of *Tryers.* This *Table* is humbly *Dedicated* by JAMES PETIVER, *Apothecary* and F.R.S.

GAZOPHILACII NATURÆ & ARTIS, TAB. XLVII.

FIG. 1. Capricornus LUZON. *maximus.* His Sheaths tawny, the reft black, Horns and Legs fhining. *Father Kamel* not only fent me the defign of this elegant Beetle, but was pleafed to make me a Prefent of the In-fect it felf.

A. 2. Ranatra *cornuta.* I firft obferved this fort in *Cain-Wood* at *Hampftead* on *Fern ftalks*, but they are not com-mon.

A. 3. Thus appears when fitting.

A. 4. Ranatra *rubra elegans, maculis nigris.* The difco-very of this beautiful Infect is owing to that nice Ob-ferver as well as Preferver of Nature, Mr *Jofeph Dan-dridge.*

5. The fame moving to fly.

A. 6. Ranatra *viridefcens.* Its *Wings* are of a faint bluifh green, and tips pale.

A. 6. *. Ranatra *fufca.* Thefe 4 laft are a new genus of Infects, approaching next to the *Locuftæ* or *Grafhoppers*, but their fhape differing: I have chofe to diftinguifh them, from their form and action, by the Name of *Frog-hoppers.*

A. 7. Its flying pofture.

8. Of-

8. Ofmunda LUZON. *repens* Fumariæ *folio. F. Kamel* amongſt his laſt *Manuscripts* ſent me this under the Title of *Fumaria capillaris.* I take it to be a *Flowering Fern,* and his Deſcription (as well as Deſign) ſeems to favour my conjecture.

9. *Asplenium* LUZON. *bicubitale pinnis alternis.*

10. *Filix* LUZON. *pinnis alternis Salici æmulantibus.* The *Leaves* of this are ſomewhat leſs waved than the Deſign.

11. Trochus LUZON. *albis maculis nigro reticulo textus.* A deſign of this and its deſcription *F. Kamel* ſent me lately in a MSS Treatiſe *de Conchyliis* Philippenſibus.

12. Millepora MEDITERRANEA. An elegant Sample of this Mr *Jezreel Jones* found lately on the *Barbary-Shoar.*

13. Cervi volantis *Caput.* Indis *Olalo.* The *Figure* and *Head* of this ſtrange Beetle *F. Kamel* ſent me.

14. Hyſterolithos *Lapis.* This wonderful Foſſil Dr *J. G. Kiſner,* a Curious Phyſician at *Frankfort,* found in the Vineyards of *Lohenſtein,* from whence Dr *John Daniel Horſtius,* Chief Phyſician to the Elector of *Heſſe Darmſtad,* formerly ſent it to *Olaus Wormius.* I have alſo received it lately from Dr *Hiegel,* Phyſician to the Elector of *Treves.*

15. Is the *Reverſe.*

To Dr PETER HOTTON, *Botanick Profeſſor* at *Leyden,* This *Table* is humbly *Dedicated* by JAMES PETIVER, *Apothecary,* and F. R. S.

GAZOPHILACII NATURÆ & ARTIS TAB. XLVIII.

FIG. 1. Fungus *Cinnabarinus* Ligni *Molavin.* an E. B. 1. 1. ſeu Act. Phil No 287. p. 1456. I. See a *deſcription* of this *Tree* in Kamel. *Syllab.* Ray V. 3. app. p. 69. 14.

2 Hemiſphericus LUZON. *Minij coloris.* This delights in the *Roſa ſine ſpinis* Kam. Ray V. 3. app. 77. i. e. *Alcea Javanica* fl. pleno.

3. Eruca *purpurea hirſuta, albis punctis notata.* This is the *Catterpillar* of the laſt Inſect.

4. Follicula *ad latera piloſa.* Thro the back of this breaks out the *Beetle* at *Figure* 2. as *Father Kamel* has accurately obſerved.

5. Cantharus LUZON. *viridis lævis. Indis* Camarinen-fium, *Dias, Giao, Lanibao,* & *Salibat.* . Both defign and Infect *Father Kamel* fent me.

6 Hæmifphœricus LUZON. *aureus maculis plurimis nigris.* This feeds on the *Garden Night fhade,* it refembles our *Common Lady-cow,* but this is larger, and has 3 times the Number of Spots.

7. Folliculus *globofus caudâ pilofâ.*

8. Erucula LUZ. *alba pilofa.* This turns into the laft which produces Fig. 6. *F. Kamel* has been very accurate in fo nicely obferving the Changes of thefe minute Infects.

9. Blatta *domeftica* LUZON. nocturna. *Hifpan.* Cucca & Cucaracha. *Lufit.* Barata. *Indis* Ipis & Bancocang. *This* refembles our *Common Houfe Cock-roach,* and like them are very devouring, and appear in the night only. The *Indians* drink their Afhes in Phyfick, they alfo bruife and mix them with *Sugar,* applying them to Ulcers and Cancers to fuppurate, it's alfo faid they are given to kill Worms in Children.

10. Corallium *ftellatum compreffum albefcens.* The fuperficies is fmooth, and the Stars fcarcely raifed. I think Mr *Stratton* brought me this from our *Weft India Iflands.*

11. Filix LUZON. *pinnis alternis ferratis. F. Kamel* calls this the *Adiatum nigrum quorundam, feu* Dryopteris *Dalechampii,* to which laft I cannot readily agree. *Ray* Syllab. *Kam.* p. 1. pl. 5.

12. Volvulaceus LUZON. *Colutaæ* foliis. *Afplenium feu Lonchitis* fcandens *Ray* Syll. *Kam.* p. 2. 15. I am apt to believe this is rather a *Bacciferous Climer* than any fort of *Fern.*

13. Cochlea *cælata,* Indis *Binga.* Under this Title F. *Kamel* fent me its defign, which is exactly copied: I take it to be a variety, if not the fame I mentioned in the *Act. Phil.* N. 274. s. S. B. 4. 22. but in this *Figure* its ftreakt Ribs and Marbled Interfticies are wanting.

14. Olivare CONDOR. *bullulis nigerrimis refertis. an* Buccinum *breviroftrum parvum nigricantibus nodis feriatim circumdatum* L. H. C. l. 4. f. 15. c. 1. Fig. 4. Tab. 954. This is an elegant fmall Shell, which Mr *Ja. Cuninghame* obferved on the Shoars of *Pulo Condore.*

15. Pectun-

15. Pectunculus CONDOR. *fasciatus undis Castaneis.* From the last place by the same hand.

16. Rhomboides *nodosus, one serrato, labro lato verruculato. an* Rhombus *parvus dentatus muricatus* L. H. C. l. 4. S. 10. c. 70. Fig. 44. Tab. 791. I have this pretty Shell in my Collection, but know not as yet from what Country.

To Dr J. G. KISNER, *Physician* at *Frankfort.* This *Table* is humbly *Dedicated* by JAMES PETIVER, *Apothecary,* and F. R. S.

GAZOPHYLACII NATURÆ & ARTIS TAB. XLIX

A. FIG. 1. Ranatra *parva pellucida Succinata.* This and the 2 next are often found in *Woods* and *Gardens,* on the shady parts of shrubby Plants.

A. 2. Ranatra *Marmorata fusca.*

A. 3. Ranatra *lata subvirens.* Those in Tab. 47. & these are most, if not all that Mr *Dandridge* or my self hath yet observed.

4. Ceterach LUZON. *scandens, pinnis alternis dentatis,* Ray *Syllab.* Kamel p. 2. 20. Indis *Panaypay.* This *Fern* has about 20 Leaves on each Stalk.

5. Ceterach LUZON. *pinnis alternis glabris.* Indis *Lagalo.* Ray *Syll.* Kam. p. 2. 19. This has 25 Leaves on each side, and is above 2 yards high.

6. Millepora AMERIC. *Spongi-arenosa.* Dr *Lewis* my hearty Friend gave me this with several other Curiosities.

7. Scarabæus LUZON. *cærulescens striatus medio cupreo.* The middle of each Sheath being Copper, distinguishes this from all I have yet seen.

8. Scarabæus *Buceros, Naficornis* primus *Kam.* Hoang LUZON. This seems very like our *Borneo* Bull-Beetle GAZ. nost. Tab. 14. Fig. 12.

9. Olivaris *nigricans, striis albis undatis.* I take this to be an *East India Shell.* 10. represents its Back.

11. Papilio *albus minor apicibus nigris.* This being tipt with black, distinguishes it from *Mus. nost.* 303. These are *Male and Female.*

12. Cus-

12. Cuſcuta LUZON. *altera ſeu major* Raij *Syllab*. Kam: pag. 1. pl. 1. Mabubu & Malobohog *Philippenſ. an* S. B. 5. 226. *Pluk.* Tab. 172. Fig. 2. H. *Mal.* V. 7. Tab. 44. p. 83. This climbs about Shrubs, and frequently on the *Agnus Caſtus* Ray V. 3. app. p. 73 3. and ,bears a ſmall tripetalous *Flower* in *April.*

13. Peĉten CONDOR. *lævis & lævis, ſupernè Caſtaneus inferne albus.* This is a very ſingular and elegant *Scallop*, being very light and externally ſmooth, the Valves within only ſtriated. The Curious Mr *Cuninghame* obſerved this with ſeveral others on the Shoar of *Pulo Condore.*

To Mr WILLIAM RAUS, Maſter of the Society ef *Apothecaries.* This *Table* is humbly *Dedicated* by JAMES PETIVER, F.R.S.

GAZOPHYLACII NATURÆ & ARTIS. TAB. L.

FIG. 1. Araneus LUZON. *longipes domeſticus.* This is a Web-ſpinning Houſe Spider.

2. Tarantula LUZON. *innocuus.* Araneus *longipes* 4. *ſeu Trojanus*. Bagna *aliis* Gambagamba *Indis.* Its *Body* as large as a *Fi bert* and brown, he lives on *Oyl-clocks*, a ſort of *Beetle.* Fig. A. Shews a flattiſh round *Silken Egg-bag,* which he carries under his Belly, which produces 1000 young ones.

3. Araneus LUZON. *telarius, argenteo, flavo & nigro tranſverſim ſtriatus.* Fig. B. is its white flat *Silk Bag,* in which F. *Kamel* thicks were 200 Eggs.

4. Araneus LUZON *longipes,* ſemini Ricino *æmulans.* F. *Kamel* hath ſent me the deligns of all theſe, with many *Obſervations* of this particular Species of Inſeĉts, which with ſome othes Traĉts of his I hope ſuddenly to publiſh.

5. Cantharis CHUSAN. *viridis elegantiſſimè variegatus.* Mr *Cuninghame* ſent me this, being one ot the moſt elegant of the Beetle kind.

A. 6. Curculio *parvus ſplendidè viridis.*

A. 7. Curculio *parvus ſplendidè æruginoſus.*

A. 8. Curculio *parvus crinitus, dorſo pallido.*

A. 9. Curculio *fuſcus, dorſo quaſi cordato.*. The 2 fiſt of theſe I have met with, the laſt are of Mr *Dandridge* his more peculiar Obſervation and not common.

A. 10. Cymecoides *virefcens*. (C) Shews its Wing clofed.

A. 11. Cymecoides *e rufo flavefcens*. I have feen thefe in *Bear, Cain* and other *Woods* about *London*.

12. Afplenium LUZON. *Ari folio*. *Phyllitis* Anglica-no Luzonis Ray *Syll*. Kam. p. 2. 18. The *Seed Leaves* are higher and more erect than the reft, ftanding on longer Footftalks than the green ones next the Root. They ufe this Plant inftead of the *Spleenwort* of the *Shops*.

13. Veneroides BARBAR. *minor marmorata*. (D.) Shews its back. *Jamaica, Barbadoes*, &c. are plentifully ftored with this Shell.

14. *Cochlea* Hortenfis *unicolor minor, umbilico parvo*. I have often met with this in *Gardens* and fometimes in *Hedges*.

To the *Reverend* Dr ALEXANDER PUDSEY, Fellow of Magdalen College.. This *Table* is humbly *Dedi-cated* by JAMES PETIVER, *Apothecary*, and F. R. S.

The 50 *Tables* to this 1 ft *Volume* of *Decades* have been pre-fented to thefe and the following Perfons, many of which have generoufly been pleafed to promife me new Subfcri-ptions towards the charge of publifhing the 2d *Volume*, near half of the Plates being already done, and will contain divers things very rare, and many of them wholly new.

TO the moft Reverend Father in God, THOMAS Lord ARCHBISHOP of *Canterbury*, Metropolitan of all England, *&c*. This *Table* is humbly Dedicated by JAMES PETIVER, F. R. S.

To the Right Reverend Father in God HENRY Lord Bifhop of *London*, *&c*. This *Table* is humbly Dedicated by JAMES PETIVER, F. R. S.

To her Grace MARY, Dutchefs Dowager of BEAU-FORT, This *Table* is humbly Dedicated by J. PETIVER.

To the Right Honourable CHARLES Earl of *Dorfet* and *Middlefex*, This *Table* is humbly Dedicated by JAMES PETIVER. F. R. S.

To Sr JOHN HOSKYNS, Kt and V. P. R. S. This *Table* is humbly Dedicated by JAMES PETIVER, F. R. S.

To the Honourable Cap. CHARLES HATTON, This *Table* is humbly Dedicated by J. PETIVER, F. R. S.

To

To Dr MARTIN LISTER, her Majesty's Physician and F. R. S. This *Table* is humbly Dedicated by J. PETIVER.

To Dr TANCRED ROBINSON, Fellow of the College of Physicians and Royal Society. This *Table* is humbly Dedicated by JAMES PETIVER, F. R. S.

To Dr HANS SLOAN, Fellow of the Colledge of Physicians, Secretary of the Royal Society, &c. This *Plate* is humbly Dedicated by JAM. PETIVER, F. R. S.

To Mr John Owen, This *Table* is humbly dedicated by JAMES PETIVER, F. R. S.

To his Grace HENRY Duke of BEAUFORT, This *Table* is humbly Dedicated by JAM. PETIVER, F. R. S.

To Mr ROB. ANTROBUS of Peter House in *Cambridge*, This *Table* is humbly Dedicated by JAMES PETIVER.

To Mr JACOB BOBART, Botanick Professor of the Physick Garden in *Oxon*, This *Table* is humbly Dedicated by JAMES PETIVER, F. R. S.

To Mr CHARLES DU BOIS, Treasurer of the EAST INDIA Company, This *Table* is humbly Dedicated by JAMES PETIVER, F. R. S.

To Mr RICH. DYER, Fellow of Oriel College in *Oxon*, This *Table* is humbly Dedicated by JAMES. PETIVER.

To MAURICE EMMET, *Esq*; Fellow of the Royal Society, This *Table* is humbly Dedicated by J. PETIVER.

To Dr RICH. RICHARDSON, Physician at *North Bierly* in *Yorkshire*, This *Table* is humbly Dedicated by JAMES PETIVER, F. R. S.

To the Learned Dr W. SHERARD, Consul of SMYRNA. This *Table* is humbly Dedicated by J. PETIVER.

To the Reverend Mr WILLIAM STONESTREET. This *Table* is humby Dedicated by JAMES PETIVER.

To Dr JOHN WOODWARD, M. D. This *Table* is humbly Dedicated by JAMES PETIVER, F. R. S.

To the Right Hon. JOHN Lord SUMMERS, Baron of EVESHAM, and President of the Royal Society, This *Table* is humbly dedicated by JAMES PETIVER, F.R.S.

To Dr HANS PET. CHARRIERE, M. D. This *Table* is humbly Dedicated by JAMES PETIVER, F. R. S.

To Mr DIXON COLBY, Master of Arts of *Merton Colledge* in OXON. This *Table* is humbly Dedicated by JAMES PETIVER, F. R. S.

To

To the Reverend Dr JOHN COVEL, Master of *Christ* College in CAMBRIDGE, This *Table* is humbly Dedicated by JAMES PETIVER, F. R. S.

- To the Honourable JOHN EVELYN, Esq; F.R.S. &c. This *Table* is humbly Dedicated by JAMES PETIVER.

To Mr PETER GELSTHORP, *Master* of the *Society* of *Apothecaries*, This *Table* is humbly Dedicated by JAMES PETIVER, F. R. S.

To Mr THOMAS GREENHILL, *Chyrurgeon*, This *Table* is humbly Dedicated by JAMES PETIVER, F. R. S.

To the Reverend Dr HEN. JAMES, Master of *Queens* College in CAMBRIDGE. This *Table* is humbly Dedicated by JAMES PETIVER, F. R. S.

To Mr E. LHWYD, Keeper of the *Ashmolean Museum* in OXON, This *Table* is humbly Dedicated by J. PETIVER.

To Mr JOHN THORPE, Master of *Arts*, of *University* College in OXON. This *Table* is humbly Dedicated by JAMES PETIVER, F. R. S.

To FRANCIS ASTON, Esq; F. R. S. This *Table* is humbly Dedicated by JAMES PETIVER, F. R. S.

To Mr JAMES AYREY, Merchant, This *Table* is humbly Dedicated by JAMES PETIVER, F. R. S.

To ROBERT BALLE, Esq; This *Table* is humbly Dedicated by JAMES PETIVER, F. R. S.

To Dr J. COATSWORTH, Physician at St *Albans*, This *Table* is humbly Dedicated by JAMES PETIVER.

To Sr GODFRY COPLEY, Baronet and F. R. S. This *Table* is humbly Dedicated by JAMES PETIVER.

To Dr PHILIP HORNECK, Physician at EXON. This *Table* is humbly Dedicated by JAMES PETIVER.

To Dr JOHN HUTTON, Physician, This *Table* is humbly Dedicated by JAMES PETIVER, F. R. S.

To Mr FRANCIS MOULT, Chymist, This *Table* is humbly Dedicated by JAMES PETIVER, F. R. S.

To Sr ISAAC NEWTON, President of the Royal Society, This *Table* is humbly Dedicated by JAMES PETIVER, F. R. S.

To Sigr. JOHN FRANCIS VIGANI, Prof. Chym. This *Table* is humbly Dedicated by JAMES PETIVER.

To Mr W. ROUS, Master of the Society of *Apothecaries*. This *Table* is humbly dedicated by J. PETIVER.

F I N I S.

A C——— —— ———
Of —— —— — —
For D————, — —— ——

GAZOPE———— ——— — —
W— ———— — —
TABLE— —— ——— ——
To which —— ———— —— ——
HOLY———— ——

By JAMES P—— —— — —
of the R——— ——

I. ENGLISH ———— ———

H———————— —— —
2 ————— —— ——
3 —————— —— —
4 ——————

5 Warty P———— ——— —
6 Lloyd's final I———— ———
7 Small ware t—— ———
8 Vernons C————— ———
9 Saffron B———— ———
10 Blue A——
11 Purple —— A——
12 Mixt A——
13 Brown ——— A——
14 Under ———— ———
15 Hairy ——— ———
16 Hair f——— ———
17 Brown ——— ———
18 Golden ——— ———
19 Checkered ———
20 Checker-like ———
21 S———— Golden ———
22 H———— ———
23 D———— work ———
24 ————

27. *Tunbridge* Grayling 14. 9.
28. *Dales* Purple Eye 24. 2.
29. *Enfeild* Eye 24. 3.
30. *Leghorn* white *Admiral* 15. 12.
31. *Gawse* Moth 44. 8.
32. *Glanvile's* Grayling 7. 8.
33. *Glanvile's* small Magpye 25. 1.
34. Shining *mottled* Moth 33. 4.
35. Mottled *Nettle* Moth 32: 8.
36. *Cambridge* Royal *Leopard* 33. 10.
37. *London* Royal *Leopard* 33. 12.
38. *Hamstead* small *Leopard* 16. xi.
39. *Ragwort* Moth 33. 6.
40. *Glanvile's* green streakt *Moth* 7. xi.
41. *Dandridge's* small greenish Moth 42. x. A.
42. *Our* small greenish *Moth* 42. xi.
43. Its *Coffin* and *Caterpillar* 42. 12. 13.
44. Hackney *Broom* Moth 14. 3.
45. *Tilman Boberts* Straw Moth. 28. 2.
46. *Glanviles* Orange girdled *Moth* 19. 3.
47. *Glanviles* Copper spotted Moth 7. 7.
48. *Our ragged* Furbelow 19 4.
49. *Glanvile's* tipt *Furbelow* 25. 12.
50. *Period* Moth 45. 13.
51. *Semicolon* Moth 45. 5.
52. Great reddish *Moth Drone* 36. 10.
53. Great brown *Moth Drone* 36. 10. a
54. Small Saffron-rumpt *Moth Drone* 42. 6.
55. Large *Hawk Drone* 36. 5.
56. Small *Hawk Drone* 42. 9.
57. Small brown girdled *Wasp* 25. 2.
58. Small, black, yellow girdled *Wasp* 25. 3.
59. Small, Saffron yellow girdled *Wasp* 25. 10.
60. Black *Hedge Fly* 14. 4.
61. Narrow *Water Spider* 9. 12.
62. Golden *Water Spider* 9. 13.
63. *Magpye* Bugg 14. 7.
64. Greenish *Bugg Kin* 50. 10, &c.
65. Marbled *Bug Kin* 50. xi.
66. Amber *Froghopper* 49. 1.
67. Brown *Froghopper* 47. 6 and 7.
68. Brown marbled *Froghopper* 49. 2.
69. *Dandridges* red spotted *Froghopper* 47. 4. 5
70. Greenish *Froghopper* 47. 6.
71. Greenish broad *Froghopper* 49. 3.
72. Horned *Froghopper* 47. 2. 3.
73. Bright green *Piper* 50. 6.
74. Bright Verdigrease *Piper* 50. 7.

75 Brown *Piper* 50. 8.
76 *Dandridges* Hart *Piper* 50. 9.
77 *Dandridges* large waved *Piper* 24. 4.
78 Scarlet small *Piper* 22. 5.
79 Blackheaded red *Piperkin* 31. 3.
80 Black horned *Comb clock* 23. 3.
81 Black pound *Comb clock* 23. xi.
82 Black ribb'd *Comb clock* 23. 10.
83 Bracken *Comb clock* 22. 4.
84 Common *Comb clock* 19. 1:
85 Hoary *Comb clock* 22. 9.
86 Green *Comb clock* 23. 12.
87 Orange girdled *Comb clock* 13. 6.
88 Slug *Beetle* 24. 7.
89 Steel *Beetle* 22. 6.
90 Common *Cow Lady* 21. 3.
91 Small *Cow Lady* 21. 4.
92 Glanviles *Cow Lady* 21. 5.
93 *Glanviles* long spotted *Cow Lady* 21. 5.
94 *Cow Lady* with 13 Specks 29. 9.
95 Hamstead *Turtle Lady* 12. 2.
96 Spotted Meadow *Turtle Lady* 29. 8:
97 Water *Flea Beetle* 13. 9.
98 Black lined golden *Beetlin* 31. 4.
99 Yellow tipt black *Beetlin* 31. 7.
100 *Russia Capricorn* 8. 8.
101 Wasp *Capricorn* 30. 4.
102 Black tipt small *Capricorn* 30. 5.
103 Small Azure *Capricorn* 31. 2.
104 *Norway* Box *Capricorn* 23. 7.
105 Orange *Feather Beetle* 23. 4.
106 Brown *Garden* Snail 50. 14.
107 *New Market* Heath Shell 17. 6.
108 *Dales* Spangle Shell 31. 5.
109 Thick *Oat Shell* 35. 6.
110 Slender *Oat shell* 30. 7.
111 Edg'd *Saucer Shell* 10. xi.
112 *Mitsham* Wrymouth 10. 8.
113 Common small *River* Shell 18. 8.
114 *Tower-ditch* Gig Shell 18. 2.
115 Double girdled *Covin* 34. 4.
116 Single girdled *Covin* 34. 5.
117 Hairy girdled *Covin* 34. 6.
118 Great *Orcade* Covin 36. xi.
119 *Dell*'s girdled *Winkle* 18. 5.
120 Wrack *Spangle* 35. 8.
121 Small Silver *Muscle* 17. 9.
122 Golden *Peak* Sattin 15. 3.

123 *Norway* Parchment Moss 14. 6.
124 *Tunbridge* Maiden-cleer 13. 4.
125 Small *Grass* Mushroom 15. 4.
126 *Cantabrick* Heath 27. 4.
127 Wallace *Orkney* Nut 34. 10.
128 *Bierly* Copper Snail 28. 10.
129 Flat *Fairy Beads* 19. 12.
130 *Stirling* Stone Moss 10. 10.
131 Rope netted *Byerly* Slate 19. 1.
132 *Byerly* black Diamond Slate 21. 2.
133 *Byerly* gritty Diamond Slate 22. 12.
134 Great *Pine Slate* 35. 9.
135 Small *Pine Slate* 35. 10.
136 Bean eyed *Slate* 18. 9.
137 Argus *Slate* 18. xi.
138 Queen Ann's *Coronation* Medal 14. 2.

EUROPEAN *Animals, Plants, &c.*

139 *Rondelets* Marble Crab 20. 10.
140 Short clawed *Lerina* Crab 20. XI.
141 Jones *Lisbon* Oyster 18. 12.
142 *Italian* Small Button Shell 17. 1.
143 *Montpelier* Button Shell 22. 10.
144 *Yorks* Snail Shell 44. 7.
145 *Wrinkled* Olive Shell 27. 2.
146 Common *Levant* Olive Shell 45. 14.
147 *Charlton's* Brimstone Butterfly 10 6.
148 Rays *Alpine* Butterfly 23. 8.
149 *Portugal* Grayling 7. 5.
150 Lisbon *Butterfly* with bloody Specks 1. 8.
151 Small *Lisbon* Tortoise Butterfly 33. 2.
152 Charltons *Montpelier* Moth 3. 3.
153 *Leghorn* Hawk Moth 12. 9.
154 *Lisbon* blue Humble Bee 12. 5.
155 *Levant* Cicada or Dew Fly 15. 7.
156 *Norway* pound Goat Beetle 2. 1.
157 Small marbled *Norway* Goat-Beetle 8. 5.
158 Yellow speckled *Norway* Piper 8. 9.
159 Lisbonne *Rhinoceros* Beetle 8. 4.
160 Slender *Levant* Mantis 28. xi.
161 *Levant* five Coral 47. 12.
162 Green *Montpelier* Thread Spunge 4. 12.
163 Four leaved *Duckmeat* 5. 12.
164 *Gallipody* Ceterac 17. 13.
165 *Paris* Spearwort 25. 4.
166 *Vailant's* least *Paris* Spearwort 25. 4.

167 *Sicilian* Spearwort 24. 9.
168 *Juniper* leaved *Campion* 34. 12.
169 *Star* Snake-wort 18. 6.
170 *Klein's* Ruffia *Muscle* 30. 1.
171 German *Hermaphrodite* Foffil 47. 13.
172 *Speners* Ring Stone 45. 12.
173 *Riga* Snail Stone 17. 3.

A S I A T I C K *Animals, Vegetables, &c.*

174 *Philippine* Centaur Monfter 45. 4.
175 *Philippine* Flying Cat Monkey 9. 8.
176 *Philippine* naked Monkey 13. xi.
177 A Bugee from *Joanna* 17. 5.
178 Small Scaly *Lizzard* 20. 12.
179 *Luzon* Guana 40. 9.
180 *Luzon* Flying Dragon 39. 2.
181 *Luzon* Calao 28. 6.
182 A *Bill* of the fame fpecies 31. 1.
183 *Chinefe* blew Bird 23. 5.
184 Strip'd Snake of *Borneo* 29. xi.
185 Scarlet *Luzon* Flying Fifh 30. 2.
186 *Luzon* Sucking Fifh 44. 12.
187 *Philippine* Soal 26. 10.
188 A Strange *Saw-like Bone* 36. 4.
189 A fmall *Square Fifh* 1. 2.
190 Marbled *Luzon* Thorney Lobfter 29. 7.
191 Greater *Luzon* Squill 43. 6.
192 Smaller *Luzon* Squill 43. 13.
193 *Great* Zeylon *Scorpion* 13. 2.
194 Flat *China* Star Urchin 36. 12.
195 Double ray'd, *China* Sea Star 4. 6.
196 Great bloody fpotted *Luzon* Butterfly xi. 8.
197 Sooty *Luzon* brown Argus 39. 4.
198 Goff's *Indian* marbled Butterfly 22. 8.
199 *Madrafs* yellow Tricolor 4. 3.
200 *Madrafs* Frittillary 40. 4.
201 Triangular eyed *Luzon* Argus 27. 5.
202 *Luzon* 7 eyed Argus 27. 6.
203 Rofe Mallow *Luzon* Argus 39. 5.
204 Its *Caterpillar* and *Coffin* 39. 6. 7.
205 White veined *Luzon* Butterfly 37. 5.
206 Blue underftreakt *Luzon* Butterfly 38. 10.
207 Yellow brown pied *Luzon* Butterfly 28. 7.
208 Yellow black edged *Luzon* Butterfly 28. 9.
209 *Goliah* Hawk Moth 8. 7.
210 Biga *Hawk Moth* of *Luzon* 40. xi.

211 Its *Catterpillar* and *Coffin* 40. 12. 13.
212 Great *Chufan* Moth 18. 3.
213 Yellow brown-ftreakt *Chufan* Moth 16 7.
214 *Smith*'s brown *Bengale* Moth 41. 10.
215 *Smith*'s greenifh *Bengale* Moth 41. xi.
216 *Smith*'s Bengale Lanthorn Moth 40. 3.
217 White *Luzon Moth* bloody edged 45. 6.
218 Black golden eyed *Luzon* Moth 43. 15.
219 Brown and white *Luzon* Moth 28. 8.
220 Its *Coffin* and *Caterpillar* 37. 2. 3.
221 Tricolor marbled *Luzon* Moth 43. 3.
222 Its *Caterpillar and Coffin* 43. 4. 5.
223 *Luzon* Beauty Moth 26. 3.
224 *Luzon* oval feathered Catterpillar 39. 12.
225 Its *Pea-like* Coffin 39. 13.
226 *Madrafs* Ring-Coffin 5. 9.
227 *Luzon* Gnat 40. 6.
228 *Luzon* 3 horned Fly 41. 5.
229 *Chufan* Thorney Cricket 39. 9.
230 Thorn Shouldered *Luzon* Bugg 40. 7.
231 Green *Luzon* Bugg 41. 6.
232 Many coloured *Luzon* Bug 41. L
233 Amber *Bugg*, with black Wings 8. xi.
234 Black *Luzon* Rhinoceros *Beetle* 44. 9.
235 *Luzon* Stag *Beetle* 47. 15.
236 *Luzon* Bull Beetle 29. 2.
237 *Luzon* Elephant *Bull* Beetle 49. 8.
238 *Borneo* Elephant *Bull* Beetle 14. 12.
249 Great *Luzon* Capricorn 47. 1.
240 Black and golden *Luzon* Capricorn 28. 5.
241 *Staphurft*'s Verdigreafe fpotted *Capricorn* 4 7.
242 Spotted *Chufan* Cantharis 50. 5.
243 *Luzon* Houfe *Cock roach* 48. 9.
244 *Luzon* Squill *Comber* 42 2
245 Speckled *Luzon* Tree *Comber* 38. xi.
246 Great Copperifh *Luzon* Comber 28. 3.
247 Dirty fpeckled *Luzon* Comber 38. 5.
248 Crack fheath'd *Luzon* Comber 26. 9.
249 Pale green *Luzon* Comber 41. 2.
250 Small *Luzon* Chefnut *Comber* 38. 6.
251 Green *Bengale* Carab 20 8.
252 Green yellow fpotted *Bengale* Carab 22. 7.
253 Green *Luzon* Carab 48. 5.
254 Grey *Luzon* Chaffer 37. 6.
255 Blew copper fpotted *Luzon* Chaffer 49 7.
256 Broad black *Luzon* Chaffer 42. 3.
257 Narrow black *Luzon* Chaffer 37. 12.
258 *Luzon* Snap-Beetle 27. 10.

259 *Bengale* green : Socker 21. 12.
260 *Luxon* green Stocker 37. 7.
261 Great *Bengale* Trumpeter 35. 5.
262 Small black *Luxon* Tumbler 42. 5.
263 *Luxon* Copper ſtrip'd *Cow lady* 41. 3.
264 *Luxon* Scarlet *Cow lady* 48. 2.
265 Its ſeveral changes 48. 3. 4.
266 *Luxon* many ſpotted *cow lady* 48. 6.
267 *Its* changes id.
268 *Luxon* Turtle Lady 9 1.
269 Its *Changes* 9. 2. 3.
270 *Smyrna* Sea Louſe 1. 4.
271 *Luxon* Bull *Crab Spider* 26. 5.
272 *Luxon* notch'd Bull *Crab Spider* 26. 7.
273 *Luxon* Moon-horn'd *Crab Spider* 26. 6.
274 *Luxon* triple Moon-horn'd *Crab Spider* 26. 8.
275 Harmleſs *Tarantula* of *Luxon* 50. 1.
276 Its Silken *Egg bag* 50. A.
277 Tricolor ſwathed *Luxon* Spider 50. 3.
278 Its white flat *Egg bag* 50. B.
279 *Luxon* Houſe *Spider* 50. 1.
280 *Luxon* ſpotted *long legs* 50. 4.
281 *Luxon* ſharp-tailed *Spider* 43. 14.
282 *Luxon* deadly Copper *Spider* 29. 4.
283 *Luxon* black leg'd *Tricoler* Spider 29. 6.
284 *Luxon* brown hairy *Spider* 29. 10.
285 *Luxon* hunch-backt *Spider* 29. 12.

A S I A T I C K *Shells.*

286 *Luxon* black girdled *Snail Shell* 32. 2.
287 Grey's *Madraſs* Sawcer Shell 1. 6.
288 *Topſy-turvy* Snail Shell 20. 9.
289 Stocker's *Bengale* ragged Mouth 4. 10.
290 Small *Perſian* Olive-Whelk 17. 4.
291 Grey's *Indian* Pot-belly xi. 6.
292 Perry's *Indian* Pap-Shell 3. xi.
293 Indian *Ear ſhell* not perforated 12. 4.
294 *Venus* Bugle 14. 10.
295 *Bengale* Bugle 20. 4.
296 *Saffron ring'd* white *Cowry* 6. 8.
297 *Buff* Leopard *Cowry* 8. 3.
298 Newt-bellied *Cowry* 5. 1.
299 Newtakin *Cowry* 12. 7.
300 Argus *Cowry* 9. 7.
301 Small notch-bellyed *blewiſh* Cowry 30. 3.
302 Small flat bellyed *blewiſh* Cowry 30. 9.

303 Saffron fpecked Cowrykin 8. 2.
304 Saffron girdled Cowrykin 8. 10.
305 Black fpeckled *Silver* Cowrykin 10. 5.
306 Black and yellow ftreakt *Madrafs* Shell xi. 3.
307 Black and white girdled *Madrafs* Olive xi. 5.
308 Black and white waved *Olive* 49 9.
309 Black *Olive* with white Specks 18 1.
310 Black warted *Condore* Olive 48. 14.
311 *Jones* bloody fpeckle girdled fmall Whelk 4. 5.
312 Chain girdled *Stamper* 15. xi.
313 *Charlton's* girdle waved golden *Stamper* 27. xi.
314 *Indian* golden girdled *Stamper* 28. 4.
315 Thick *Madrafs* Stamper 19. 5.
316 Warty *Madrafs* Stamper 19. 10.
317 *Luzon* Leopard *Stamper* 47. xi.
318 *Luzon* Fair-wing 48. 13.
319 Broad *Hoof* Stopple 4. 9.
320 Narrow *Hoof* Stopple 4. 8.
321 *Madrafs* reddifh *Stopple* 16. 3.
322 Warty *Indian* Stopple 28. 12.
323 *Borneo* Ear-cap 21. xi.
324 Smooth *Condore* Scallop 49. 13.
325 *Luzon* Duck-bill 32. 9.
326 *Luzon* Hammer Oyfter 45. 3.
327 *Madrafs* furrow-waved *Tellen* 13. 8.
328 *Madrafs* fmooth waved *Tellen* 16. 9.
329 *Madrafs* broad-headed *Tellen* 19. xi.
330 Undulated *Condore* Purs 48. 15.
331 *Indian* Venus Cockle 31. 9.
332 *China* crefted *Balanus* 6. 10.

ASIATICK *Herbs, Shrubs, Trees,* &c.

333 Blew fpeckled *Luzon* Coral 10. 12.
334 Purplifh *Luzon* Spunge Coral 31. 8.
335 Bloody *Luzon* Spunge Coral 31. 12.
336 Double netted *Luzon* Fan 32. 1.
337 *Luzon* Nett-ball 32. 3.
338 *Luzon* Furze Coral 35. 12.
339 *Luzon* Gozo 27. 12.
340 Ship *Pipe-wrack* 9. 6.
341 *Luzon* Scarlet *Agarick* 48. 1.
342 *Madrafs* Wrack Mofs x. 1.
343 *Luzon* Penny-Fern 48. 12,
344 *Luzon* round cut *Fern* 4. 4.
345 *Luzon* Saw-Fern 48. xi.
346 *Luzon* Willow-Fern 47. 10.

347 *Luzon* Protean *Fern* 20. 3.
348 Great *Luzon* Willow *Ceterac* 49. 5.
349 Small *Luzon* Willow *Ceterac* 47. 9.
350 *Luzon* Crooked *Ceterac* 14. 1.
351 *Luzon* Heart *Ceterac* 50. 12.
352 *Luzon* notcht *Ceterac* 49. 4.
353 *Luzon* Fumitory *Osmund* 47. 8.
354 Fine veined *Madrass* Pondweed 31. x.
355 Fine veined *Madrass* Yam 31. 6.
356 *Madrass* Pellitory *Blite* 31. xi.
357 *Luzon* Rue Teasel 20. 1.
358 *Madrass* Agrimony 32. 10.
359 Small *Madrass* Motherwort 32. 12.
360 *China* Livelong *Crowfoot* 12. 3.
361 *China* Orange *Crowfoot* 19. 6.
362 *China* Arrow-head 19. 5.
363 *Malabar* netted Cucumber xi. 2.
364 *Madrass* Bastard *Clovewort* 5. 8.
465 *Madrass* Grass *Birdsfoot* xi. 11.
366 *Madrass* Penny *Birdsfoot* 26. 1.
367 *Madrass* joynted *Birdsfoot* 26. 4.
368 *Madrass* Penny *Lentils* 33. 1.
369 *Madrass* hairy *Lentils* 30. xi.
370 *Madrass* hairy *Rattle-broom* 30. 10.
371 *Surat* Melilot 10. 1.
372 *Madrass* pied *Kidney beane* 21. 8.
373 *Madrass* Bezoar *Kidney-bean* 21. 9.
374 *Genseng* 24. 8.
375 *Chusan* Androsace 33. 8.
376 *Luzon* Doso 19. 7.
377 *Luzon* Bontian 44. 10.
378 *Luzon* Ticala 18. 7.
379 *Zerumbet* 23. 3.
380 *Cassamuniar* 27. 1.
381 *Encalades* Amomum 20 2.
382 *Kamell's* Amomum 41. 8.
383 *Zedoary* 23. 1.
384 *Turmerick* of *Kamel* 37. 9.
385 *Madrass* Grass *Schananth* 2. 6.
386 *Chusan* Hare *Grass* 36. 1.
387 *Luzon* Dodder-berry 49. 12.
388 *Telle molle* 16. 1.
389 *Oriental* Anacardium 40. 14.
390 *Viziagapatan* ball 22. 1.
391 *Luzon* Balanti-Tree 43. 1.
392 *Chusan* Nut-berry 36. 7.
393 *Luzon* Brittle Tree 43. xi.
394 *Garcias* his *Caranda* of *Kamel* 44. xi.

395 *China* Carambola 37. 8.
396 *Luzon* Champacca 24. 1.
397 *Luzon* Quince leaved Chaft Tree 34. xi.
398 *Coffee of Pemet* 46. 9.
399 *Chufan* Cyprus 6. 3.
400 *Luzon* Date-like Stone 38. 3.
401 *Chufan* Virginia Sumack leaved *Fagara* 36. 8.
402 *Hobom* Nut and Kernel 45. 7. 8.
403 *Luzon* Wormwood *Jafmin* 42. 7.
404 *Surat* Kermes 2. 8.
405 *Kamel's* Kernel 42. 4.
406 *Necklace* Kernel 38. 4.
407 *Macer* of the *Antients* 20. 5.
408 *Manile* Mananingtang 19. 8.
409 Girdled *Luzon* Marble Nut 37. xi.
410 *Naican* Briftle Nut 42. 8.
411 White netted *Naican* Nut 42. 14.
412 Great *Balete* Nutmeg 42. 10.
413 *Panguaguafon* a Counter-poyfon 45. 1. 2.
414 *Luzon* Pofopolo 43. 2.
415 *Chufan* Berry Rofe 35. xi.
416 Blue *Japan* Elder Rofe 36. 2.
417 Common *Rottang* 39. 10.
418 Great *Rottang* 39. xi.
419 *India* Snakewood 42. 1.
420 *China* Tallow Tree 34. 3.
421 *Malabar* Tavacare 16. 4.
422 *Madrafs* Tavacare 16 5.
423 Common *Tea* 21. 10.
424 A Chair of its *Roots* 21. 1.
425 Scarlet *Rofe* Tea 33. 4.
426 *Chufan* Laurel *Whorts* 35. 7.
427 Black *Luzon* Zapotle 43. 7. 8. 9. 10.
428 Scarlet *China* Zapotle 45. 9. 10. xi.
429 *Chinefe* Mayz Stone 30. 8.

AFRICAN *Animals, Vegetables,* &c.

430 Great *Cape* Shrew Moufe 23. 9.
431 Plume-tail'd *Cape* Crane 12. 12.
432 *Cape* Cardinal or *Red Bird* 10. 7.
433 *Cape* yellow headed *Humming Bird* 7. 9.
434 *Cape* Silver *Snake* 16. 12.
435 *Cape* Tricolor *Snake* 10. 3.
436 *Cape* Philamort *Butterfly* 9. xi.
437 *Cape* Dew Fly 4. 1.
438 Yellow *Cape* Locuft 3. 6.

439 *Cape* Feather Legs 12. 1.
440 Yellow *Cape* Tarantula 12. xi.
441 *Cape* Mole Locuft 13. 7.
442 Black and Orange *Cape* Beetle 8. 6.
443 Black furrowed *Cape* Beetle 24. xi.
444 Black *Cape* Slug Beetle 12. 6.
445 Hoary fpeckled *Cape* Comber 8. 6.
446 Great *Cape* Centipes 13. 3.
447 Blufh *Cape* Hippuris 3. 10.
448 Warty *Cape* Wrack 9. 14.
449 Porous *Cape* Rainbow *Mufbroom* 4. xi.
450 Ruyfch's *Cape* Cudweed 7. 1.
451 Small fpiked *Cape* Cudweed 8. 12.
452 *Cape* Comofe *Silver Tufts* 7, 3.
453 *Cape* ear'd *Silver Tufts* 30. 12.
454 *Cape* double white *Straw Flower* 1. 9.
455 *Cape* fingle Blufh *Straw Flower* 5. 10.
456 *Cape* clammy headed *Knapweed* 25. 6.
457 *Cape* Knapweed with Woolly Grafs Leaves 6. xj.
458 *Cape* *Maudlin* with Samphire Leaves 34. 1.
459 *Cape* foft leaved *Herman* 34. 2.
460 *Cape* Purple *Dyers broom* 5. xi.
461 *Cape* Myrtle *Cone* 6. 4.
462 *Cape* Pine *Cone* 25. 7.
463 *Cape* headed *Breynian* 8. 1.
464 *Cape* hoary headed *Breynian* 5. 4.
465 *Cape* Heath *Breynian* 5. 2.
466 *Cape* fpiked *Breynian* 3. 9.
467 *Cape* red flow er'd *Heath* 3. 7.
468 *Cape* Cotton headed *Heath* 2. 9.
469 *Cape* mouldy headed *Heath* 2. 10.
470 *Cape* Time Lewifan 5. 7.
471 *Cape* Thorny *Spindle Tree* 26. 2.
472 *Guiney* Pompom or Bugle Lizzard 15. 6.
473 Black *Guiney* Butterfly with white fpots 3. 4.
474 *Kirckwood's* fpeckled *Angola* Butterfly 9. 5.
475 *Kirckwood's* Selvidge eyed *Angola* Butterfly 6. 9.
476 White *Angola* Butterfly with bloody Tips 9. 10.
477 *Skeen's* brown pied *Butterfly* 12. 10.
478 *Planer's* yellow *Guiney* Moth 29. 3.
479 Nonpareil girdle bodied *Guiney* Moth 33. 7.
480 Briftle tail'd *Mount Serado* Fly 2. 4.
481 Sprinkle winged *Aleppo* Alderboult 3. 1.
482 Small *Aleppo* ftreak'd Beetle 2. 12.
483 Hairy fpeckled *Aleppo* green Beetle 13. 5.
484 Warty *Wida* Unicorn Shell 5. 5.
485 Flat *Afcenfion* Balanus 9. 9.
486 Bloody wafted *Barbary* Mufhroom 39. 8.

487 *Barbary* Wild Oats 38. 7.
488 *Barbary* Glasswort 40. 2.
489 *Barbary* Ragwort 41. 4.
490 *Barbary* blush *Carline* 38. 12:
491 *Barbary* whorle leaved *Teafel* 41. 7.
492 *Barbary* notch leaved *Feverfew* 40. 5.
493 *Barbary* naked *Daify* 40. 1.
494 *Barbary* Sea Lavender 41. 12.
495 *Barbary* small *Star Fig* 39. 3.
496 *Barbary* like *Bindweed* 40. 10,
497 *Barbary* white *Broom* 37. 13.
498 Sweet yellow *Barbary* Milkwort 41. 9.
499 Saw-leaved *Barbary* Dwarf Ciftus 38. 9:
500 Purple *Barbary* Broom Rape 37 4.
501 *Barbary* Dwarf-like *Aloes* 40. 8.
502 *Barbary* Fox Grape 39. 1.
503 Yellow *Barbary* Spurgewort 38. 8.
504 Boccones *Barbary* Thorn 29. 1.
505 *Guiney* like *Nutmeg* 38. 1.
506 *Guiney* Myrtle xi. 7.
507 *Guiney* Hare Grafs 2. 7,
508 *Guiney* Taggee 17. 10.
509 *Guiney* pierc'd Wood Nut 37. 10.
510 Common *Abrus* 44. 1.
511 Great *Anacock* 44. 4.
512 *Canary* Orchili 7. 12.
513 *Palma* Pellitory 7. 2.
514 *Smyrna* Reaper, a Sculpture 16. 2.

AMERICAN *Animals, Vegitables,* &c.

515 *Carolina* Bull Frog 25. 5.
516 *Maryland* blue tailed *Lizzard* 1. 1.
517 *Maryland* blue chin *Lizzard* 14. 8.
518 *American* white spotted *Snake* 6. 5.
519 *American* Ribbond *Snake* 46. 1.
520 An Ear tufted *Water Fowl* 43. 12.
521 *Maryland* Flame Throat 3. 8.
522 *Maryland* yellow Throat 6. 1.
523 *Surinam* Bill Bird 44. 13.
524 *Surinam* Red Cap 46. 12.
525 *Surinam* yellow Cap 46. 13.
326 *American* Toad Fish 20. 6.
527 *Brazil* spotted *Barbel* 20. 7.
528 *Carolina* Sea Loufe 1. 3.
529 *Barbadoes* Star Egg 5. 3.
530 *Williams* yellow tipt *Carolina* Butterfly 7. 10.

531 *Wil.*

531 *Bohuns* yellow fpotted *Carolina* Butterfly 6. 12.
532 *William's* Orange girdled *Carolina* Butterfly 15. 9.
533 *Williams* Selvedge eyed *Carolina* Butterfly 33. xi.
534 Jones *Maryland* Selvedge eye 2. 3.
535 *Virginia* Painted Lady 33. 5.
536 Black *Darien* Butterfly with 2 white Spots 6. 7.
537 *Mexican* Butterfly with 2 Scarlet blots 4. 2.
538 *Jamaica* Tricolor 13. 1.
539 *Vincent's* large *Surinam* Peacocks eye 28. 1.
540 *Vincent's* Surinam long *Tricolor* 12. 8.
541 *Charlton's* Copper bliftered *Surinam* Butterfly 10. 9.
542 Small blue *Surinam* Butterfly 46. 15.
543 Greenifh *Maryland* large *Page* Moth 14. 5.
544 *Maryland* long *Crofs Moth* 17. 7.
545 *Maryland* fhort *Crofs moth* 17. 8.
546 *Maryland* Ermin moth 17. 2.
547 *Maryland* Buff Ermin Moth 3. 2.
548 Golden Lanthorn *Carolina* Butter Moth 32. 5.
549 Great *Carolina* Lanthorn Bee Moth 32. 7.
550 *Maryland* mottled Bee Moth 17. 12.
551 *Carolina* Twig Coffin 7. 6.
552 Feather horned *Carolina* Fly 6. 6.
553 *Virginia* Wingless Wafp 13 10.
554 Clear tipt *Maryland* Adderbolt 15 1.
555 Cloud tipt *Maryland* Adderbolt 15. 2.
556 *Mexican* Bull Rhinoceros 46. 14.
557 Brown *Maryland* Bull Rhinoceros 24. 10.
558 *Campeachy* Goat Chaffer 24. 6
559 *Bohun's* brown fpeckled *Goat-chaffer* 25. xi.
560 *Maryland* Wafp Beetle 27. 3.
561 *Carolina* Wafp Cantharis 33 9.
562 Copper fpotted *Maryland* Carab 2. 2.
563 Velvet eyed *Virginia* Snap Beetle 10. 4.
564 Marfhal's *Virginia* Chaffer 27. 7.
565 Green *Maryland* Chaffer 27. 9.
566 Green *Maryland* Horn Chaffer 27. 8.
567 True *Cochineel* with its changes 1. 5.
568 Great *Maryland* Cow Lady 33. 3.
569 Straw *Maryland* Cow Lady 26. xi.
570 Yellow and black ftreakt *Maryland* Beetle 17. x.
571 Speckled *Barbadoes* Rag Oyfter 24. 12.
572 *American* rugged Hart Henckle 25. 9.
573 *American* ridged Hart Henckle 24. 5.
574 *Jamaica* pointed Henckle 25. 8.
575 *Dominico* Tellen 18. 4.
576 Flat *Jamaica* two tooth'd Shell 21 6.
577 *Barbadoes* Lady Whelk 22. xi.
578 *Stoneftreets* flet Pap fhell 3. 12.

579 *Car-*

579 *Barbadoes* Lattice pied *Nerit* 13. 12.
580 *Barbadoes* Partridge *Nerit* 10. 4.
581 Small *Jamaica* Saffron mouth'd Nerit 15. 8.
582 Common *American* Olive 9. 4.
582 *Barbadoes* Net Olive 30. 6.
583 Hollow twirl'd *Nevis* Unicorn 46. 7.
584 *Barbadoes* Diper 50. 13.
585 *Barbadoes* Ring Shell 15. 5.
586 Strattons *American* Star Coral 48. 10.
587 Lewis *American* Sand Pore 49. 6.
588 Robinfons *American* Spunge Pore 23. 2.
589 Strattons *Barbadoes* Spunge Coral 23. 6.
590 *Virginia* Orack *Silver Tufts* 7. 4.
591 *Maryland* Randal wort 6. 2.
592 Krieghs *Maryland* flender *Plantain* 1. 10.
593 Flat *Barbadoes* Abrus 44. 5.
594 Long *Antego* Abrus 44. 2.
595 Long *Antego* Scarlet Abrus 44. 3.
596 *Jamaica* Magpye *Kidney bean* 38. 2.
597 Yellow *Maryland* Star Pimpernell 2. 5.
598 *Carolina* ground *Flax* 5. 6.
599 *Vigo* Betle 46. 6.
600 *Mexican* Chocolate *Betle* 46. 5.
601 True *Vanilia* 46. 2. 3. 4.
602 Blue *Virginia* Water Hyacinth 1. 12.
603 Yellow *Virginia* Grafs *Star Flower* 1. xi.
604 *Maryland* Winckle berry 1. 13.
605 *Pomets* Peruvian Bark 49. 9. x. xi.
606 *Mexican* Tulip claw 46. 8.
607 *Carolina* Turtle Foffil 46. 16

ADVERTISEMENT.

HAving now finifh'd my *Firft Book* of *Decades*, and given you here a *Claffical and Topical Catalogue* of them, I am now by feveral *Perfons* perfwaded to proceed to another *Volume*, and for the fatisfaction of *New and Re-fubfcribers*, I have 30 *Tables* ready to deliver to each *Perfon* that depofits a *Guinea*, and in hopes of fpeedy *Encouragement*, will publifh the reft with all Expedition.

An *Addition* to my *Hortus Siccus* in the *Appendix* to *Mr Ray's* 3d Volume of *Plants* p. 241.

Bengale Plants from *Mr Bulkley.*

1. Ægylops *Bengalensis* glumis pilosis aureis
2. Arundo *Bengalens.* purpurea
3. Amourettes *Bengal.* paniculis majoribus
4. Amourettes *Bengal.* paniculis minoribus
5. *Ricinus* Bengal. *Persicæ* fol. aspero
6. *Malva Rosea* Bengal. *Aceris* fol. fl. pleno
7. Lathyrus *Bengal.* angustifol. purpureus
8. Phaseolus *Bengal.* siliq. tetragonâ fimbriatâ
9. *Intsia* Bengal. *Abrus* folio, Siliquâ curtâ
10. *Intsia* Beng. *Mimosæ* fol. *Senæ* Siliquâ longiore
11. Waga Beng. fol. minimis Siliquâ longâ
12. *Cocculus* Bengal. *Castaneæ* folio triphillo.

Cochinchina Plants from *Mr Cunninghame.*

13. *Lingua Cervina* Cochinchinensis *Ophioglossi* facie
14. Lonchitis *Cochin.* latifolia florida
15. Lonchitis *Cochin.* perelegans nodiflora
16. Adiantum *Cochin.* pectinatum ramosissimum G. N. 70. 12:
17. Adiantum *Cochin.* majus segment. acutioribus
18. Filix *Coch.* ramos. scand. pinnis eleganter squamosis
19. *Juncus* Cyperoides *Cochin.* fol. argenteis
20. Adrachne *Cochin.* spinosus
21. Pimenta *forte* Cochir. *Calambac* à nonnullis putata
22. Kadali *Cochinchin.* tetraphilla
23. Kadali *Cochin.* fol. ferrugineo holosericeo
24. *Castanea* nucleo oleoso, Dow-tein *Coch.* dicta
25. Carambola *Annanamica* fructu venenoso
26. Aurantium sylv. *Annanamica* fol. molli
27. Baccifera *Cochin.* Suberis folio

Condore Plants from *Mr Cunninghame.*

28. Hædysarum *Condoriæ.* Phaseoli fol. subtus glauco
29. Dracontio affinis *Condoriæ.*
20. Kadali *Condor.* Cinnamomi fol.
21. Evonymus *Condor.* spinosus Citrii fol.
22. Moschata *Condor.* sylv. fr. ferrugineo
23. Rhus *Condor.* fructu triquetro
24. Sassfras facie. Arbor *Condorica*
25. Arbor *Condor.* fol. bifido pulchrè venoso
26. Arbor Pixigradendros D. *Cunningham,* vulgo *Damar Tree* or *Tarr Tree,* Dampier 391
27. Baccifera carinata *Condor.* Lauri folio

Smyrna

Smyrna Plants from *Dr Sherard, Conful of* that Place.

28 Ophioglossum *Smyrn.* minimum fol. *Gramineo* G. N. 73. 6.
29 Gramen Tremulum *Smyrn.* annuum spicatum
30 Gr. *Secalinum Smyrn.* annuum ariftis longiffimis
31 Gr *Smyrn.* cap. ex utriculo prodeunte cornutum G. N. 73. 5.
32 Plantago *Smyrn.* pilosa minima G. N. 73. 3.
33 Tithymalus *Smyrn.* hirfutus
34 After *Smyrn. Pfeudo Dictamni* folio
35 Scabiosa *Smyrn.* montana repens hirfuta
36 Horminum *Smyrn.* Lampfanæ fol.
37 Thymbra *Smyrn* lignofa *Rorifmarini* folio
38 Convolvulus *Smyrn.* fol. angulofo hirfuto, fl. albo
39 Lepidium *Smyrn.* glauco fol. caulem ambiente
40 Tragacantha *Smyrn.* fol. in spinam abeuntibus
41 Genifta *Smyrn.* humilis argentea fl. albo
42 Cytifus *Smyrn.* fl. luteo minimo. fil. brevi glabra
43 Lotus *Smyrn.* argent. lutea, humifusa, rad. craffa
44 Vicia *Smyrn.* paluftris glabra, fl. candidis
45 Ciftus *Smyrn.* humilis, Oleæ fol. fl. luteis
46 Lychnis *Smyrn.* mont. *Spergulæ* folio
47 Lyfimachia *Smyrn.* fpicat. *Luteola* fol.
48 Hexapetala *Smyrn.* tricapful. fl. albo. rad. fibrofâ
49 Thymelea *Smyrn.* mont. repens, fol. anguftiff. fl. carneis
50 *Thymelea Sm.* mont. cefpitofa *Kali villof.* fol. glauco, fl. carneis
51 Chamæmefpilus *Smyrn.* fol ferrato fub ûs lanuginofo

Carolina Plants from *Mr Job Lord,* &c.

52 Juncus inutilis *Carol* polycephalos
53 Lactuca *Carol* hirfuta
54 *Hieracium* Carol. *Pilofellæ* folio
55 *Hieracium* Carol. *Behen alb.* folio
56 Tragopogon *Carol.* fl. minore
57 After *Carol.* Cyani fol. integro
58 Cirfium *Carol.* purp. Limonii folio
59 Jacea *Carol.* purp. fpicata *Limonii* folio
60 *Jacea* Carol. purp. fpicat. *Limon.* fol. hirfuta
61 *Jacea Carol. Salicis* fol crenato
63 *Chryfanthemum* Carol. *Limonij* folio
64 Chryfanthemum *Carol.* haftato folio
65 Chamænerion *Carol.* fol. & fl. minoribus
66 *Carambu* Virg. *Eruca* fol. hirfuto
67 Cytifus *Marianus* luteus *Anil.* folio
68 *Kadali* Carol. *Hyperici* facie hirfuta
69 Cyftaneæ Equinæ fol. *Carol.* fl. coccineis
70 Frutex fpicatus *Carol.* Sumach dictus
71 Ricinus *Carol.* Quercus minoris folio
72 Spiræ facie *Americ.* Ariæ folio
73 Styrax *Carol.* fl. majore *Ellis*
74 Styrax *Carol.* fl. minore *Ellis*
75 — — con *Carol.* Juinbæ folio *Ellis*

Place
3. 6.

1. 73.

eis
carnes

..

Lightning Source UK Ltd.
Milton Keynes UK
UKHW01f0634021018
329873UK00005B/431/P